HOW – WHY – WHERE

3 Questions That Must Be Answered Before You Die.

Thiz book had knot bin proffesionaly editted on puropose cause' I don't want know gramar Natzi takin' away none of the pheel of this first-purson written prospective or add eny "big" words to the manewscript. So, pleese half grayce win on this voyedge wit me!!

Ok, did you just cringe from the above? Sorry about that!

This book is dedicated to you.

It took me many years to write this because tackling 3 of the biggest questions man has ever faced in under 100 pages was difficult. But I wanted you to not feel like reading this was going to be too big of a task. I thought of and prayed for you the whole time.

ISBN:

Table of Contents

Foreword
Alex McFarland _____ Page 04

Pieces
From My Life's Journey _____ Page 07

HOW
Did We Get Here? _____ Page 20

WHY
Are We Here? _____ Page 65

WHERE
Do We Go When We Die? _____ Page 49

CONCLUSION
What Does This Ultimately Mean? _____ Page 82

www.DaveGlander.com

FOREWORD
Written by Alex McFarland

Dave Glander reminds me of a Bible verse.

I should probably phrase it this way: *A certain Bible verse reminds me of Dave Glander.*

Knowing Dave's ministry of apologetics, you might assume the Scripture to which I refer is First Peter 3:15 (a verse commonly associated with a rational defense of the Christian faith). Maybe you're thinking about Jude 3— which speaks of "earnestly contending for the faith" (which Glander faithfully and effectively does).

Knowing Dave as I do, plenty of other inspiring verses come to mind when I think about all that he stands for and what God does through this man's ministry (II Peter 1:16-21; Philippians 1:17; Matthew 24:35; Psalm 19; *et al*).

But if I had to pinpoint a single verse that I think Dave Glander personifies, it would be Matthew 22:37. Here Jesus Christ sets forth the *summum bonum* for every human's life: "Love the Lord your God with all your heart and with all your soul and with all your mind." Life's greatest blessing is to know God personally. Having received the gift of salvation through faith in Jesus Christ, we are to love and serve Him with our emotions, will, abilities, and intellect.

More than 30 times in the Old Testament similar injunctions appear, calling people to love the Lord with heart, soul, and mind. Usually, this call of the whole person to God is accompanied with the admonition that Jesus repeated in Luke 4:8, ". . . *and Him only shall you serve."*

Many today mock the Biblical worldview. But in this year that has seen everything from riots, vandalism, to endless political rancor and character assassinations, we are in dire need of more knowledge of the distinctly *Christian* view of reality. Even famed atheist Richard Dawkins (who, in an email, once called me a "flat earther" for believing in God), said in his book **Outgrowing God,**

"Whether irrational or not, it does, unfortunately seem plausible, that if somebody sincerely believes God is watching his every move, he might be more likely to be good."

Jesus had a lot to say about beliefs and behaviors. He invited all people to put their faith in Him and experience His special plan for your life. And regarding our beliefs, that is our "worldview," Christ promised, "You will know the truth and the truth will set you free" (John 8:32)

In the book of Proverbs chapter 23, verse 7, the Bible states "As a man thinks in his heart, so is he . . ." Centuries after this was written, modern psychology would concur, noting that that *thoughts* begat actions, and of course, actions and behaviors shape our personal destinies and outcomes.

What we think about— or assume to be true— can even influence our health and can help or hurt relationships with others. What we believe definitely informs / determines our relationship with God.

A light of truth in a worldview wasteland

Nowadays it is highly frowned upon to critique anything others believe. In fact, you can lose your career for doing this. A single tweet or social media post deemed "inappropriate" by God-hating, politically-correct, internet "thought police" can be used to destroy a person. Courageous people today *must* speak up . . . because viewpoints and ideas have consequences.

In February of 2020, chart topping rap artist DaBaby— commenting on the impact of Facebook, Twitter, TikTok, Instagram, *et al*— said that social media is all about, "lost souls, influencing lost souls." Famously left-leaning Comedian George Carlin is said to have stated, "Political correctness is fascism pretending to be good manners."

When I think of someone who (from my perspective, at least) has totally invested himself in all that is Christianity— holding back nothing— I think of Dave Glander.

As a representative for Jesus, Dave is at the same time radical in obedience and yet meticulous in his handling of truth. I am so glad that Dave's story is presented in this book! I am also glad that readers will benefit from Dave's extensive knowledge of apologetics.

Like myself, Dave Glander believes that people of all ages (especially young people) need to be aware of the compelling *evidences* for Christianity. For as long as I have known him Dave has excelled in presenting the evidences for Christianity in a compelling way— and this book is no exception.

Imagine how much brighter the light of the Gospel would shine in our nation today if more believers were like Dave Glander in their passion to defend truth! I urge people to read Dave's book, and most importantly, follow his example. For God's glory, I intend to!

A brother in the Gospel,

www.alexmcfarland.com

PIECES
From My Life's Journey

Picture the scene from the movie, "A Christmas Story," where the dad was in the basement cursing at the inoperable furnace. The wife just sat there listening to vulgarities fly out of the dad's mouth... *"ReesaFrackaWhockaShoooby Haka Dango Bing Bong!!!"* Well, if you can picture that, then you also just witnessed what was apparently the moment I met God! Yep, that was the night I came back to my house and unleashed on a God whom I didn't even think existed. To say I was mad at the way my life was turning out was a bit of an understatement. I screamed straight through the ceiling and roof of my house at this imaginary God and asked him what kind of a god would he be to create somebody and then leave them to live a life of complete turmoil? I cursed him out while crying so hard that snot was pouring out of my nose and mixing together with the gallons of tears flowing from my eyes. I was mad, frustrated, worn out, hopeless, and empty. But how did I get to such a point where suicide seemed like a much better option than to face another single day in misery?

My life's journey hasn't always been the prettiest story ever told. I couldn't have been more than 2 or 3 years old when it started. I really can't quite remember with vivid details the beginning of when my uncle began to molest me, all I know is that by the time I was starting to become a child, my childhood innocence had already been robbed, and the abuse continued until I was at least double-digits. For those who have had similar experiences with sexual abuse, you know how it can take a toll on your moral compass if you don't get help. Needless to say, I kept it a secret for so long that I allowed it to become a part of who I was; it was a part of who I identified as; I was a victim. To make matters worse, a life of drug abuse began when I was only six years old (yes, I said six...). I guess some neighborhood teenagers thought it would be funny to get me and my friend to drink some Coca-Cola laced with actual cocaine and topped off with sniffing rush (a quick massive rushing high). All I remember is running out the front door of that house and jumping off the front porch screaming, "whoooohoooo!" Those same two teenagers also got me started smoking cigarettes. By the time I was seven years old, I was buying my own packs of cigarettes through my older friends. Yep, as you can see, I wasn't off to the greatest start in my journey through life. It became part of my identity. I was already living a life under the radar from my parents.

I smoked my first joint when I was twelve years old. By the time I was sixteen I would travel to Central Park, in New York City, to purchase large quantities of LSD (Acid), and return home to sell it for fairly good profits. At the same time, I was also eating enough of the acid myself to kill a horse. I dropped out of school by the age of 16 and made selling marijuana and acid my identity. Truth be told, the 7th grade was the last grade I technically completed. I was "advanced" [thrown out] of the 8th grade to get me out of the school because I caused so much trouble. My first attempt at 9th grade ended with only about 130 days of attendance, and my second attempt only gathered around 40 cumulative totals.

Growing up in New Milford, Connecticut, I can only remember a handful of churches anywhere around. Most of them were Catholic, with a couple Methodist here or there. In the time that I spent growing up in New England, the overall environment was pretty void of any "religion" at all. There were some yuppie kids who attended a private Catholic school at the top of the hill in downtown. We all made fun of them because they really weren't very nice. Other than them, I can't really remember any other version of Christianity anywhere. While certainly warmed by the awesomeness of my mom, my home wasn't a Christian home in any ways. The only time I heard the name Jesus Christ was when my dad was yelling at something… he certainly wasn't in praise mode at all☺. I suppose it was all of this lack of God that ultimately led me into becoming an unbeliever. Living everyday as though there is no accountability to anyone, or anything was who I was; it was my identity; I was an atheist.

I moved to the Bible-belt when I was eighteen years old. I was in a bit of a culture shock to see a church on nearly every street corner. I saw cars with Christian stickers plastered on them driving around like idiots giving other drivers the "you're #1" sign. I overheard Christians talking smack about other Christians while sipping coffee. And let me tell you something… when you wait tables and see a bunch of sharp-dressed Christians coming in after church, you know one thing for sure – you're about to get NO tip from them at all (waiters/waitresses, can I get an amen?!) Because I didn't grow up with a lot of Christians around, I was watching every move they made, and most weren't making good moves. I guess that's when I turned militant in my atheism; I really didn't like Christians at all. That was my identity. I was now a militant atheist.

I remember a time when I was selling cars and the used car manager invited me to a bible study. For whatever reason, I was so offended by the offer that I literally lit into the dude and asked him what kind of nerve he had asking me to participate in such utter nonsense. [As I just wrote that, I can't help hearing Jim Carey as the Grinch saying in my head, ***"The Audacity! The Nerve!"***] (did I mention I have A.D.D. ☺) Standing next to the manager was one of the sales guys that attended these bible studies. After I got done chewing the sales manager out, the sales assistant walked with me outside and calmly, and respectfully, asked me one of the most profound questions anyone had ever asked. He said, *"If you don't believe in God, then what do you believe?"* For the next hour and a half, we walked around the car lot as he listened to me talk a mile a minute about all of my theories about life. I babbled, and babbled, and babbled, and babbled, and babbled, and babbled, on and on, and on and on, and on about NOTHING at all! I confused the crap out of myself so badly that when I finished talking, I really had no idea what I had just said. That poor guy! If you think I was confused, you should've seen the look on his face. He just kind of blankly starred at me and said, *"Ok, well I've got to get back to work."* That poor guy had no clue how to respond to the gobbledygook I just got done spewing out of my clueless mouth. Man, up until that point, I thought I was this really deep person who, through the use of many drugs, had come up with the theory of life that explains everything. I lived as though I thought I knew everything, and that no one else had the wisdom to figure out. My identity had been of being a guru that knew what life was all about. Boy did I have egg on my face after that parking lot conversation.

And The Walls Came Crumblin Down!

My mom was my absolute best friend in the whole wide world. She was my rock that I could turn to no matter what I was going through. For many years I battled self-worth problems that led me to live a life of depression, which is why I ultimately stayed as high as possible through life. I could call my mom at any point in time and she was always there to listen first, give great advice second, and always leave you chuckling before you hung up the phone.

On one eerie day, I got a phone call that I will NEVER forget, as long as I live. My dad called me and said that mom is sick; really sick. The doctors had found a mass in her abdomen that was causing great swelling and the prognosis was not good. I swear, within minutes, I was in my van heading to Florida! The next day I went into the doctor's private office with my mom where she was about to be given the diagnosis. The doctor held his hands apart a few inches and said that they found a mass. I looked him dead in the eye, held up my own hands, and asked, *"mass, or MASS"* [as I moved my hands further apart]. He moved his hands further apart and said, *"MASS."* Have you ever felt like all of the sudden, the room you are sitting in begins to grow, leaving you with the feeling of being a tiny speck of dust in the corner of a massive room? Well, you understand how I felt.

A few weeks later they took her in for surgery to attempt to remove the mass. She was supposed to be in there for several hours, but after only 45 minutes, they came out to let us know that she was inoperable. She was given about 3 months if she could have a bowel movement, or about 3 days if she could not. I've never wished for poop before in my life, but on that day, I was sure hoping for some poop. At that time, I had long dirty blonde/brownish hair, skinny with a young attempt at a beard. As I walked into the hospital cafeteria this dude sitting with a big group jumped up and yelled, "*HE'S RETURNED!!!*" The rest of the people he was sitting with immediately burst into laughter. It took me a few seconds to realize that he was making a funny about me looking like Jesus. In full disclosure, I went through a phase where looking like Jesus seemed like the best way I could mock the whole idea of Jesus. Inside, when that guy made that funny, I was so proud to have been the vessel that caused laughter [mocking] about Jesus. Funny side note that I'm thinking about while writing… I remember leaving that cafeteria and going into the hospital chapel. There was no one there and I had no clue what you're supposed to do in there, so I just sat there for about 15 minutes in silence thinking about how sad I was for all that was going on. If only I'd have known then what I know now…

Fast forwarding, my mom managed to make it about a year. I left all my responsibilities at home and basically moved to Florida for a huge portion of the time when she was going through chemo and stuff; and I don't regret a second of that decision. Time is like money. You can spend it any way you want, but you can never get it back. The time I got to spend with my mom was bittersweet. On the one hand, there were some awesome moments of pure joy, but on the other hand, I saw some things that can never be unseen. Things I have barely ever repeated to anyone. Things that only my precious grandma, Debbie (oh Debbie, how important you were at that time), and my dad know about. As I write on this exact day, it has been 17 years since the day that my mom died.

A day or so before she left, she gave me a nugget that I still carry to this day. In the days before she died, she was basically in a state of complete unconsciousness. One by one, we each took turns going into the room where she was to tell her it was o.k. for her to go. When it was my turn I went in, held her hand, and told her not to worry about me; that I would be o.k. I swear to you on what I'm about to share that it is as true as it comes. My mom woke up, looked at me with the most lucidly clear eyes I had seen in weeks and said, *"Shoot! I know you're going to be fine. You're going to have one HONEY of a life ahead of you, that's part of the reason why I don't want to go. I don't want to miss it!"* And then just like that, she fell right back into the coma-like unconsciousness as she was a few seconds earlier. As an atheist, I didn't know where to file that incident. All I knew was that it was almost supernatural in nature (something I didn't allow for at the time), but I'll tell you what... it changed my identity a bit. All of the sudden it was like I had something to look forward to; something totally unknown and exciting all at the same time. For the first time in my life, my identity was faced with the possibility of the eternal.

Well, before things could get better, I had to make them worse. My dear friend John was at the jobsite doing some sheetrock work when I got back to Georgia after the funeral was over. He knew how utterly broken I was and offered me a bump of cocaine. Now, besides the incident when I was six years old, I had somehow managed to avoid cocaine, heroin, PCP, meth, etc... But on that day in my worst moment of weakness, I was ready to see what the hype was all about. I needed some relief from where my depression was starting to go after the reality was kicking in that I would never be able to talk to my mom again. I bent over that bathroom counter and hit my first line of cocaine. For whatever reason, it had little to no effect on me. A few days later I tried it again to no avail. The third time he offered me a bump, I thought to myself, *"if it doesn't work this time, then I give up."* I bent over a dryer in the basement of this house and snorted a huge line this time. Immediately I grabbed my nose and screamed! John started to laugh and told me that I'd be feeling this for the next 30 plus hours! It wasn't cocaine this time; it was Crystal Meth – ICE. For the first time in a long time, I felt incredible! I felt like I was ready to conquer the world. The thing about drugs is that they don't last forever! You have to keep feeding your body the intoxicants in order to keep your feelings and emotions where you're trying to get them. It's a false feeling. A horrible mask that gets uglier as time goes on. Over the next 3 plus years of my life, I was an addict... that was my new identity.

I would like to take a moment and share a poem with you, written by a young woman named, Alicia Van Davis, about Crystal Meth. She wrote this while in jail on drug-related charges, and I'm here to tell you, she absolutely nailed it.

My Name is Meth

I destroy homes, I tear families apart,
Take your children, and that's just the start.
I'm more costly than diamonds, more precious than gold,
The sorrow I bring is a sight to behold.
If you need me, remember I'm easily found,
I live all around you – in schools and in town.
I live with the rich; I live with the poor,
I live down the street, and maybe next door.
I'm made in a lab, but not like you think,
I can be made under the kitchen sink.
In your child's closet, even in the woods,
If this scared you to death, well it certainly should.
I have many names, but there's one you know best,
I'm sure you've heard of me; my name is Crystal Meth.
My power is awesome; try me you'll see,
But if you do, you may never break free.
Just try me once and I might let you go,
But try me twice, and I'll own your soul.
When I possess you, you'll steal and lie.
You'll do what you have to – just to get high.

The crimes you'll commit for my narcotic charms
Will be worth the pleasure you'll feel in your arms.
You'll lie to your mother, you'll steal from your dad,
When you see their tears, you should feel sad.
But you'll forget your morals and how you were raised,
I'll be your conscience; I'll teach you my ways.
I take kids from their parents, and parents from kids,
I turn people from God, and separate friends.
I'll take everything from you, your looks, and your pride,
I'll be with you always – right by your side.
You'll give up everything – your family, your home,
Your friends, your money, and then you'll be alone.
I'll take and take, till you have nothing more to give,
When I'm finished with you, you'll be lucky to live.
If you try me be warned – this is no game,
If given the chance, I'll drive you insane.
I'll ravage your body; I'll control your mind,
I'll own you completely; your soul will be mine.
The nightmares I'll give you while lying in bed,
The voices you'll hear, from inside your head.
The sweats, the shakes, the visions you'll see,
I want you to know, these are all gifts from me.
But then it's too late, and you'll know in your heart,
That you are mine, and we shall not part.
You'll regret that you tried me; they always do,
But you came to me, not I to you.
You knew this would happen, many times you were told,
But you challenged my power and chose to be bold.
You could have said no, and just walked away,
If you could live that day over, now what would you say?
I'll be your master; you will be my slave,
I'll even go with you when you go to your grave.
Now that you have met me, what will you do?

Will you try me or not? It's all up to you.
I can bring you more misery than words can tell,
Come take my hand, let me lead you to hell.

At the young age of only twenty-one years old, Alicia died from a Crystal Meth overdose.

After a while, meth had taken over my life. My house was in foreclosure status. My car was repossessed. I quit my job. I moved out of my home where my wife and son were still living and moved into a dead man's estate before it sold. It was a cold, empty house that had a broken waterbed in one bedroom, a broken computer, and that's about it. I managed to find some old couch cushions on the side of the road to create a make-shift bed in the corner of what was supposed to be a dining room. I had withered away to about a hundred and ten pounds. I was hanging out in places that I'd rather not discuss, with people that I hope you'll never know. I was basically a withered away homeless guy who had let life get the best of him. That was my identity. That's what I owned as myself. If I had had gun at the time, I would've most certainly killed myself. However, I was afraid to try any other method for fear of failure. I was afraid if I tried to overdose that I would fail and look stupid for not being able to take enough of the right drugs to finish the job. I was afraid that if I stepped in front of a semi-truck that I would end up failing and becoming a paralytic for the rest of my life. I was afraid to fail at committing suicide, which is failure itself. I was afraid to fail at failing; that was my identity... I was a failure.

What do you do when you think there is no ultimate purpose for your life, and you've managed to destroy what life you did have? I had no idea what to do, except to go home to where my wife was after 9 long months of being gone. She graciously let me in where I proceeded to go through where I started this chapter.

(Go re-read the first paragraph of this book – Did you do it? For goodness sake, go re-read it so we can pick up where it left off! Alright, now we can move on...)

After I got done cursing out a God that I didn't even believe in, I said these magic words; this was my alter call moment. I said to Him, *"If you're* **GOD,** *then* **DO SOMETHING** *about it!!!"* My wife then got me some tissues and put me to bed. Truth be told, I probably hadn't slept in weeks because of the meth addiction. What happened next is where things really start to get interesting. I woke up the next morning completely changed. The meth addiction was gone completely!!! It was as if I had never done meth a day in my life. I had absolutely no urge to get high at all. I couldn't even remember what it was like to feel high! Yes, you should be cheering right about now because that DOES NOT happen like that, EVER! Most of the time you have to either go to a rehab, take methadone to come down off the addiction, or quite simply, you don't make it at all. I can't tell you how many people I've seen die because of this drug. God DID SOMETHING about it! Not only was the meth gone, but there was so much different about me that I didn't understand what was going on.

Houston, We Have A Problem

I knew that something "supernatural" must have happened to me, but I couldn't comprehend that. Up to that point, the supernatural couldn't exist in my purely naturalistic evolutionary worldview that I had had all my life. I had a major problem on my hands. What if I actually experienced a touch from God? Heck, there was no room for what if. For the first time in my life, I KNEW there was a God, but who was He? And did He change my identity?

Over the next few months, I started to research which god did this to me. I wanted to find out the truth about the supernatural because I became convinced that one of the alleged gods was responsible for my radical life change. A radical life change that I personally did nothing to make the change. I simply reached out to this unknown God and asked Him to do something in my life before I ended it permanently. And this God didn't ask me to change for Him, no. By His grace and love alone, He saw it fit to reach down to me first and heal my life. I had to find out who did it so I could properly thank Him for doing such a miraculous thing to me. I had to find an answer to my NEW Identity!

The first possibility for god I looked into was Buddha. I found out that he was a real person that lived about 600b.c. He was a prince that was heir to his father's throne. He was basically caged inside the kingdom for his entire youth where his parents told him that everything in the world was always perfect, and that no suffering existed. One day, Sidharth Gautama (the Buddha), escaped the palace and went adventuring into the common land. There he saw poverty, malnutrition, hate, violence, etc. He was taken aback by everything he was seeing and found a fig tree to sit under in order to meditate on what reality actually was, for he now knew that what he was taught for his entire life was a lie!

As endearing as that story was to me, here's where my search for the Buddha being the one responsible for my change came to an abrupt halt. Gautama was raised in the traditional Samkhya, which is a Hindu school of thought that historically had no place for a god. That's right; the first rule in Buddhism is that there is essentially no need for a god. Now, I'm not saying that Buddha was an atheist, but when you live your life as though there is no Creator, then that essentially makes you either an atheist, or at least an agnostic. Either way, the fact was that Buddha couldn't be god since he didn't even believe in a God! This obviously made him a non-contender for my life change. The other reason why I couldn't accept Buddhism as a possibility was due to the fact that the sayings of Gautama weren't physically written down for nearly 600 years after his death. That's way too much time between events to ensure that anyone could know what was being taught was the same as what was being written down as Buddhist doctrine. There's a great possibility that hearsay, legend, rumors, etc. would have infiltrated the Buddha's teachings.

The next candidate for a possible god to me was Allah. I remember exactly where I was, and what I was doing on the day that America was hit with the greatest act of terror on our mainland that we had ever seen. On September 11, 2001, four commercial airliners were hijacked using box cutters. One of those planes was intercepted by the passengers on the plane who were able to overtake the terrorists enough to crash in an empty field. One of the planes managed to be flown straight into the Pentagon in Washington, D.C. But it's those two planes that were flown into the World Trade Centers that was plastered on every news channel that really grabbed my attention. Even though at the time I was an atheist, I was very impressed by the zeal these Muslims had for their faith. So fast forward to when my search the alleged god began, I remembered 9-11 and thought that it must be Allah who did it. I certainly hadn't witnessed any other religion, especially Christianity, exhibit such amazing fanaticism for their belief – surely it must be true! Surely their god must be the one was responsible for my new identity.

Well, everything was going just fine in my research about Islam at the beginning. I learned that the founder of the faith was named Muhammed. He was born in the city of Mecca in 570a.d. He worked as a shepherd in his early years until he went to work as a traveling merchant with his wealthy cousin, Khadija. After a few years as business partners together, Khadija asked Muhammed to marry her; and he accepted. Appalled by the new materialism and idolatry in Mecca, Muhammed hiked into the mountains into a cave where he received visions from a supposed angel. These visions instructed him to recite the words that eventually became the holy book of Islam known as the Quran (Qur'an).

As intriguing as this search for Allah was going, I discovered some information about Muhammed's visions that I found absolutely disturbing. When he received his first vision, it shook him so badly that he wanted to commit suicide by throwing himself off the cliff where he had been meditating.[i] As a matter of fact, Muslim tradition holds that Muhammed made many attempts at committing suicide, but was stopped each time by the supposed angel, Gabriel.[ii] If that's not bad enough, the reason why Muhammed wanted to kill himself was because he knew that his own people, the Quraysh Tribe, would think he had been possessed by a demon! I even found the references in their own holy book, where they refer to Muhammed being a *"bewitched man deprived of reason and influenced by magic."*[iii]

Stop the presses! I'm sorry, but when I was looking for the truth about the God who changed me, I encountered a major belief issue. Any religion created by a crazy man who thought he was so possessed by a demon that he attempted suicide multiple times and had to be convinced by his cousin-wife [Khadija] that his visions were really from God, could NOT possibly be true! There was absolutely no way that I was going to believe that this irrational religion was the explanation for my radical encounter. This on top of the fact that Muhammed finished his life in bloody battles and said that Allah had told him to conquer the world by slaying massive amounts of people and forcing them to accept Islam as their god. That rational had nothing at all to do with the love I felt from whatever God was responsible for my new identity.

This led me to research the last place I thought I'd find the truth, Christianity. What you will read in the following pages is a culmination of my journey to find the God who changed my life when I thought I was beyond any version of hope that could be found. Sit back, relax, and enjoy the ride. My A.D.D. (not sure about the "H" – they didn't have that letter when I was diagnosed many moons ago) may take us down some rabbit trails at times, but I promise if you stay on the ride you too will find life, hope, and purpose in the truths I'm about to share with you. If I haven't already told you; I love you. I know you'll see that as you read along...

HOW

Did We Get Here In The First Place?

Alright. Hang with me on this chapter. Yes, there will be some discussion about "Science," which may not excite all of us (I hated the study at one point in time), but when you get past that and into the meat of this chapter, you will find yourself enthralled in the world of the amazing creation of life, and it will reveal a portion of who you are in this quest for the meaning of life!

When I was very young my mom asked me where babies came from, and my response until I was around 10 years old was, "*McDonalds!*" When asked more directly, I would say, "*They came out of the mommy's leg.*" As farfetched as these options may sound, they sounded a lot more feasible to my finite young mind than the scenes of Storks dropping swaddled babies from the sky that gracefully landed on the front porch of a joyous family. I guess it may have been my fear of falling that deterred me from the Stork, so giving birth from your leg at a McDonalds obviously sounded better to me. Laugh as you may, but what sticks out about this memory is that from a very young age, I had a theory about how we all got here. As a matter of fact, every thinking person since the beginning of time has had to ask themselves how we all got here. The question of our origins is vitally important to our understandings of why we are here at all. The truth of our origins can impart an eternal perspective about our ultimate purpose in life.

To simplify the question of how we all got here in the first place, we are going to go ahead and address the only two options out there that attempt to explain how man came to be on earth. There are no other options; only two. Not ten, not five, not three; only two. First is the Theory of Evolution. Second is what's referred to as, "Special Creation." Either the Universe can be seen as an explanation of unguided formation (evolution), or something beyond the Universe is necessary to explain the complexity of life (special creation). I will give a brief explanation of how each of these positions work, and then give reasons why only one of them truly satisfies the question of how we got here.

Option 1: The Theory of Evolution

The Theory of Evolution has roots in Ancient Greece and Rome, where the idea is that species change over time. In the early 19th century, Jean-Baptiste Lamarck (1744 – 1829) proposed his theory of the *"transmutation of species,"* the first fully formed theory of evolution. The theory made a gigantic leap in popularity when Charles Darwin published *"The Origin of Species,"* which has become the cornerstone of modern evolutionary models. The main component to Darwinian Evolution is a mechanism called, *"Natural Selection."* Darwin claimed that we all came from one single species that emerged out of a gooey pond in the beginning. From that single-cell species, billions of mutations occurred until another totally distinct species emerged. Then another, then another, then another. Then those species mutated so that they caused other completely different species from these mutations. Darwin called the illustration of evolution, *"The Tree of Life."* Picture the base, or trunk, of a tree. Move up the tree and you'll have branches that come from the single base, and then each one of those branches have smaller branches coming off of them. The further along you go, the more branches you have, but all from the one single base (trunk) of the tree. And that is how everything got here according to Darwin.

Before we move on, there's something that has always bugged me that most truthful scientists will agree upon. That is, the complexity of life emerging spontaneously, without guidance is nearly impossible! Francis Crick, the noble prize [atheist] who co-discovered DNA said this about our origins, *"An honest man, armed with all the knowledge available to us now, could only state that in some sense, the origin of life appears at the moment to be almost a miracle, so many are the conditions which would have had to be satisfied to get it going.*"[iv] Scientists realize how much it takes to form even the simplest of life structures. Are we then supposed to believe that while this process of creating new species was happening (as impossible as it seems to do once) is simultaneously happening to create both a male and a female at the same time in order to guarantee reproduction and survival of this new found species? So not just one near impossible event, but two at the same time! That's just too implausible for me to believe…

It is a scientific fact that *"Micro"* Mutations occur within the DNA sequence of all living cells. These mutations can be triggered by things like radiation, viruses, mutagenic chemicals, and even in the cell replication process. According to Darwinian evolution, these micro-mutations are exceedingly small, tiny occurrences that are completely accidental by nature, and are completely blind and unguided. Basically, there is absolutely no force at work behind these random mutations; they are purely natural only. Here is where the cornerstone of Natural Selection comes into play. After these blind, accidental, unguided, and random micro-mutations occur, Natural Selection chooses which micro-mutation is most beneficial to the survival and reproduction of the species.

A simple example that is often used by teachers of evolutionary theory is the difference between two different color beetles. The argument goes like this: a random, blind, accidental micro-mutation occurs in the coloration of a Beetle's spawning process, causing both brown and green beetles to be created. Since the green beetles are prettier, through the process of Natural Selection, a bird will choose to eat the green beetles over the brown beetles. Because all the green beetles were eaten by Natural Selection (aka: the Bird), the mutated brown colored beetles won the chance for domination and survived, whereas the mutation of the green colored beetle lost. The more advantageous trait of brown coloration allows the beetle to have more offspring, which becomes more common in the population. If this process continues, eventually, all individuals in the beetle population will be brown.

There are two basic concepts that are essential to the failure of this argument. One is that we can all observe the overwhelming myriad of different colored beetles around the globe. I remember going to a museum a few years ago where they had what they called an "*Insectarium*." There were literally hundreds of iridescent beetles of all different colors on display, in a multitude of shapes and sizes. Now, if the example of the brown and green beetle held any weight at all, there really should only be a limited coloration of beetles in existence, especially given the millions of years that evolution claims to have available for these mutational occurrences to have been naturally selected. However, the observable evidence we have available tell a different story altogether. The hundreds of examples I saw looked more like an artist hand-painted them in all of their diversity. Even though insects and I don't get along at all, I couldn't help but stand in awe of their beauty. Maybe it was also because they were dead and behind glass that eased my tensions.

The second challenge to the green/brown beetle argument is that preference to a beetle's color is completely subjective to each particular bird. It has been studied that birds can see colors that are invisible to the human eye because of additional color cones in their retina that are sensitive to ultraviolet range. How does the evolutionist know that a bird thinks green is prettier than brown? Isn't it more likely that just like humans, choice of color preference is subject to the individual bird? I'm speculating here a bit, but I'm sure there are some birds who hate the color green, which is why saying that green bugs are less likely to survive due to Natural Selection is just a poor argument in general. We will discuss the processes of Darwinian Evolution throughout the rest of this section, so we will end that segment of our class today and move to the second option that attempts to explain how we got here in the first place.

Option 2: Special Creation

Special Creation states that the universe, and all life in it, originated in its present form by a special force which preceded the creation itself. Special Creation seeks to recognize from observable evidence that point to intelligent design, which is the opposite of evolution's random, blind, unguided, accidental process. Special Creation recognizes that there are fingerprints of a Grand Artist found throughout the entire universe. From the microscopic nucleus of a cell, to an interstellar nebula, Special Creation makes the argument that it is necessary to accredit a supernatural being for creating everything we see. There are two areas of thought that combine here that need to be defined. First, by using the word *"Special,"* we are indicating that what we actually find through observable science is unique and different than what we would expect to find from random accidental processes of evolutionary theory. Special means that we find better and more important design features than what should be expected. Think about it, can blind accidentally spilled paint ever arrange colors into patters that could form the Mona Lisa? No, it takes an artist to arrange the sequence of colors in order to create a work of art. No amount of time and chance could ever arrange random, accidental drops of paint onto a canvas that would form anything coherent, like the works of Leonardo da Vinci. What special is really referring to is the idea that there is a Grand Artist at work who has displayed a massive amount of thought and intelligence in His creation. This area of study is what is known as *"Intelligent Design."* Second, the word *"Creation"* means that there is an emphasis on the Bible as a reference point to explain what we are finding in our scientific ventures. Now, don't confuse that as using the Bible to explain scientific observations; that would be Bible validates Science (even though there are dozens of examples that could actually be mentioned here). No, what we are doing is observing the evidence available to us, then turning to the Bible to see if our finding undeniably matches up; that is Science validates the Bible (aka: Creationism). So, when we put the two words together, *"Special Creation,"* simply means Intelligently Designed observations within Biblical Creation. Now that we have outlined the foundational principles of each of the two options, let's take a look at what the observable sciences show us.

The Theory of the Beginning of Life

I remember sitting in my science class hearing the well-meaning teacher discuss common ancestry; the idea that chimpanzees and humans came from a common ancestor. Every time this theory came up, I found myself less concerned about the common ancestry aspect of how we got here, but more concerned with how did anything at all get here in the first place? You see, back when Darwin wrote the Origin of Species the question of origins hadn't really been addressed. Instead, he focused solely on common ancestry, not biology as it pertains to beginnings. But hold on! Don't attempt to tell me I came from a line of common primate; I want to know how the primate got here in the first place! I let that question rest for many years until the question of origins really needed to be faced if I was going to answer the question of HOW we got here. My studies immediately took me to a field of study called, *"Abiogenesis."* According to the Merriam-Webster Dictionary, the meaning of Abiogenesis is as follows; *"a theory in the evolution of early life on earth: organic molecules and subsequent simple life forms first originated from inorganic substances."*[v] So, in my quest for truth, I began to research this theory.

It was only in the 17th century that magnification technology reached a point where scientists could examine what makes us up. As microscopic sciences advanced, physicist Robert Hooke discovered what he coined as, *"Cells"* in describing biological organisms, which became known as *"Cell Biology"* [aka: Cell Theory]. Cell Theory looked at the nature of cellular regeneration, and the idea of cells as a fundamental unit of life. Cell Theory has become the cornerstone for modern biology and is the most widely accepted explanation to the function of cells. There are three scientific statements that define the cell theory:

1) All living things are composed of one or more cells.
2) Cells are the basic life structure of a living thing or organism.
3) All cells come from pre-existing cells through reproduction.

Alas, I have hit the jackpot on my search for HOW we got here. Forget the common ancestor, we've gone way past that back to the question of origins and found out that it's all about Cells! Ok, now that I know what makes up every living thing, I just have to figure out HOW the cell got here in the first place. It seems as though this question of HOW is very illusive! How did the first cell get here?

I'm going to take you on a journey, far, far away, to the land of the unknown! That's right... the unknown. You see, in the beginning, none of us were there. There's not a scientist who has ever contributed to any field of science that was there in the beginning. There are also no theologians who were there either. Not a single human being can give an eye-witness testimony to what actually happened during the first moments of time. The best we can do is take the information available to us now and try to formulate the best rational explanation for what happened in the past. On this journey, we are going to attempt to explain how the first cell could have formed. Then, we can look to see if that possibility can explain HOW we got here.

Grandma's Famous Cake vs. The Cell

Cells are remarkably complex entities. Before we get into the complexity of a single cell, let's examine what it takes to form a cell from scratch. Ok, picture making a gloriously delicious cake from scratch that you got from Grandma's famous recipe box. You would start by gathering all of the necessary ingredients from the recipe list. Then, you would methodically follow Grandma's instructions on how to assemble the ingredients one-by-one, in the exact order. Next, you would carefully bake the cake in the perfect environment to ensure that it will rise correctly and retain the textbook level of moisture. Finally, you'd have to time the production process perfectly in order to not overcook the cake and render it useless for consumption *{I'm starting to get really hungry!}*. After a strict period of cooling off, you can now apply the icing to the cake. You're almost there... now it's time to prepare the creation for transport to Grandmas without damaging it (you didn't think you could have your cake and eat it too, did you?). Viola, you've done it! Now, think about that same process as it applies to creating a cell, only a trillion times more difficult.

The first question you have to ask yourself is this; Could that cake have randomly, accidentally, and blindly created itself [magically appeared] without any intervention at all?

You just cried out, "*NO*" in your head as you read that last question, didn't you? That's because you are a logical person, and you understand that things just don't randomly create themselves blindly. You are actually probably patting yourself on the back for being a baking genius because you made Grandma proud. You used your intelligence to create that glorious cake! What if you had a blindfold on while making the cake, could you have done it? Even more extreme, what if you just threw all of the ingredients up in the air and caught them in a bowl that landed in the oven; do you think the cake would turn out perfectly? Again, I hear you screaming a resounding, "*NO*" in your mind at the absurdity of these ideas.

However, that is exactly what it appears the evolutionists would have you believe about the creation of a cell, which again, is so much more complex than a cake that it's hard to wrap our minds around.

The Ingredients for Cells (Life)

Using the illustration of the cake example we just looked at, I'm going to walk you through the process of creating a single living cell. The very first step in creating a cell is to create a correct Amino Acid (like flour for the cake), which is the cornerstone in creating a living cell.

Chemical Evolution is the theory that claims to answer HOW the first cell spontaneously appeared from non-living chemicals. Supposedly, in the beginning, the Earth was covered in nothing but a giant cesspool of inorganic (non-living) chemicals that is assumed to have contained the correct ingredients [recipe] for life to emerge. Some refer to this initial state as a pre-biotic (warm) soup, or goo. At some point in the Earth's existence, something like a lightning charge, meteorite, deep-sea hydrothermal vents, or an electric discharge from the sun struck the warm soup at just the right time and Viola, you had a single Amino Acid! While this theory had its roots in the early 1900's by a Russian atheist named, Alexandr Ivanovich Oparin, it didn't really take shape until a team from the University of Chicago made it famous in 1953. Led by his mentor, Harold Urey, a scientist by the name of Stanley Miller had accomplished what the scientific community had long been waiting for; the creation of the first step of life (amino acids) in a test tube.

The Miller/Urey experiment was an attempt to recreate the earth's early atmosphere in a set of glass tubes. On the lower left portion of the glass tube apparatus there was boiling water which represented the "warm" ocean. The boiling water caused water vapor to rise through a long vertical tube, and then turn down another tube and into a chamber that held gases that Miller ***assumed*** were present on the earth's original atmosphere. Once the water vapor and gases [namely methane, ammonia, and hydrogen] mixed together, continuous electrical sparks were fired to simulate lightning into the water vapor. Next, the simulated atmosphere was cooled again so that the water condensed and dripped down into a collection trap at the bottom of the apparatus. From there, Miller quickly removed the "dark goo" that had collected in the trap. Contained within the goo were a few amino acids, which Miller claimed to support the theory of the beginning of life.

So, does this solve the possibility that life could have emerged by purely natural processes? To answer this question, we have to look at the integrity of the experiment, and then compound that with the complexity of what the next steps of creating a cell are.

Let's go back to grandma's glorious cake illustration again. You see, grandma gave you the right ingredients to make a perfect cake. You had a predetermined set of instructions that set you up for success. It wasn't like you had to put on a blindfold and start rummaging through your kitchen cabinets pulling out random items to use in your cake. No, you kind of cheated by using a recipe that you KNEW would work best. In the same manner, Stanley Miller kind of cheated by using a mixture of chemicals that he KNEW had the ability of creating an amino acid. This immediately begs the question – did Miller use an accurate chemical mixture that would have been present in an accurately simulated early atmosphere? As a matter of fact, most all of modern scientists would agree that he did not! Like grandma's recipe for success, Miller cheated the system by using a recipe he knew would work. He knew that by using a simulated atmosphere heavy with primarily hydrogen, ammonia, and methane, he stood a high probability of successfully manufacturing amino acids. But was there a methane–ammonia atmosphere present at all on earth's early atmosphere? In his book, **A Science Odyssey: 100 Years of Discovery**, Dr. Flowers says, *"... the accepted picture of the earth's early atmosphere has changed: It was probably Oxygen-rich with some nitrogen, a less reactive mixture than Miller's, or it might have been composed largely of carbon dioxide, which would greatly deter the development of organic compounds."*[vi]

Wait a minute! A giant elephant just appeared in the room with that last statement by Flowers; Did he just say Oxygen-rich? If that's an accurate hypothesis of the earth's early atmosphere, then why did Miller use an oxygen-free environment to conduct his experiment? The answer is really quite simple; Miller KNEW that oxygen would destroy any organic material that he was able to produce. For example, when we die, we decay. As a part of the decaying process, oxidation of the body causes destruction of organic materials, generating carbon dioxide and water. Miller knew that if he allowed the probability of oxygen in the simulation, he wouldn't have been able to manufacture any organic amino acids; **he cheated!** The bottom line is that Stanley Miller used ingredients that he knew could work, while forsaking the integrity of what science should be; honest. What's more is that Miller used *Intelligence* in formulating his rigged experiment to produce anything at all, which flies in the face of evolutionary models that claim there is no intelligence behind our existence. Evolutionists only allow for a blind, accidental, and unguided process that sets up the possibility for natural selection to perform its function. I'm sorry, but what Miller knowingly did is an unacceptable and downright unprofessional scientific practice! It throws logic out the window for the sake of trying to supplement a result that Miller needed to support his theory.

A Scientific Sidenote

The definition of science has changed to suit the everlasting desire of the evolutionist's attempts to satisfy their theories. If you were to go to the original Webster's Dictionary of 1828, you would find the following definition of science:

SCI'ENCE, noun [Latin scientia, from scio, to know.]

1. In a general sense, knowledge, or certain knowledge; the comprehension or understanding of truth or facts by the mind. The science of God must be perfect.

2. In philosophy, a collection of the general principles or leading truths relating to any subject. Pure science as the mathematics, is built on self-evident truths; but the term science is also applied to other subjects founded on generally acknowledged truths, as metaphysics; or on experiment and observation, as chemistry...[vii]

Did you catch acknowledgment of God as the author of science? Did you also happen to catch the application of *"Metaphysics"* as a valid addition to the scientific method? Metaphysics is defined as, *"the branch of philosophy that deals with the first **principles of things**, including **abstract concepts** such as **being**, knowing, substance, **cause**, identity, time, and space."*[viii] (Emphasis added is mine)

The modern definition of science has since changed to:

*A: knowledge or a system of knowledge covering general truths or the **operation of general laws** especially as obtained and tested through scientific method*
*B: such knowledge or such a system of knowledge concerned with the **physical world** and its phenomena.*[ix] (Emphasis added is mine)

No longer is the concept of metaphysics allowed in scientific study. ONLY naturalistic explanations are allowed to color the outcome of experiments. Basically, the pre-conceived bias of evolutionary science has rendered the possibility of the super-natural to be completely forbidden. The evolutionist is making the claim that there absolutely cannot be a God, and this principle affects how they perceive known factual evidences. Now, add to this that scientists like Miller don't even practice a genuine level of scientific integrity to conduct experiments, then how are we supposed to know the truth about our origins if modern science has used lies to produce their results, and they've removed God as a distinct possibility for what we know to be true?

It is a well-known fact that God held His rightful place at the beginning of modern science. When science was originating into its current form, men of great intellect sought to answer the questions about the nature of God through close examination of His creation. The upcoming list could be as long as this whole book if all of the contributions to early science from Christians were listed. I have included just a short list of names that most people will recognize. Their contributions have shaped our understanding of our universe, and they were all die-hard Jesus freaks:

- **Francis Bacon** (1561–1626): is credited with establishing the inductive method of experimental science via what is called the scientific method today.
- **Galileo Galilei** (1564 –1642): an Italian astronomer, physicist, engineer, philosopher, and mathematician who played a major role in the scientific revolution during the Renaissance.
- **Blaise Pascal** (1623–1662): well known for Pascal's law (physics), Pascal's theorem (math), and Pascal's Wager (theology).
- **Robert Boyle** (1627–1691): prominent scientist and theologian who argued that the study of science could improve the glorification of God. A strong Christian apologist, he is considered one of the most important figures in the history of Chemistry.
- **Isaac Newton** (1643-1727): prominent scientist during the Scientific Revolution. He was a Physicist, discoverer of gravity, an alchemist, and an obsessed Christian apologist who was obsessed with trying to discern the date of the Rapture from the Bible.
- **Johannes Kepler** (1571-1630): prominent astronomer of the Scientific Revolution. He discovered Kepler's laws of planetary motion.
- **Gottfried Leibniz** (1646–1716): he concluded that our Universe is, in a restricted sense, the best possible one that God could have created. He also made major contributions to mathematics, physics, and technology.
- **Albrecht von Haller** (1708–1777), Swiss anatomist, physiologist known as "the father of modern physiology.
- **Antoine Lavoisier** (1743–1794): considered the "father of modern chemistry". He is known for his discovery of oxygen's role in combustion, developing chemical nomenclature, developing a

preliminary periodic table of elements, and the law of conservation of mass.
- **Alessandro Volta** (1745–1827): Italian physicist who invented the first electric battery. The unit Volt was named after him.
- **William Whewell** (1794–1866): professor of mineralogy and moral philosophy. He is the wordsmith who coined the terms "scientist," "physicist," "anode," "cathode," and many other commonly used scientific words.
- **Michael Faraday** (1791–1867): known for his contributions in establishing electromagnetic theory and his work in chemistry such as establishing electrolysis.
- **Lord Kelvin** (1824–1907): did important work in the mathematical analysis of electricity and formulation of the first and second laws of thermodynamics.
- **George Washington Carver** (1864–1943): scientist, botanist, educator, and inventor. Carver believed he could have faith both in God and science and integrated them into his life. He testified on many occasions that his faith in Jesus was the only mechanism by which he could effectively pursue and perform the art of science.

According to "*100 Years of Nobel Prizes*," a review of Nobel prizes award between 1901 and 2000, reveals that (65.4%) of Nobel Prizes Laureates, have identified Christianity in its various forms as their religious preference.[x] Overall, Christians have won a total of 72.5% of all the Nobel Prizes in Chemistry, 65.3% in Physics, 62% in Medicine, and 54% in Economics.

There is no lack of intelligence and contributions to science from the Christian community. Again, the above list was merely a portrait of a much larger force of scientists who helped shape what we know about the world we live in. Science was never opposed to God, as it is circulated now. On the contrary, science was initiated by Christian scientists who were enamored with the fingerprints of the God of the universe! Therefore, I must conclude that the pride of man may have caused arrogant scientists to remove God from the equation, looking for merely naturalistic explanations for the scientific method. Not only did they change the definition over time, but a myriad of fraudulent claims have been documented that all show a lack of integrity coming from the evolutionist's side. All you have to do is study claims like the Piltdown Man, Haeckel's embryo drawings, Peppered Moths, and the Mysterious "Feathered Dinosaur" and you'll see that the lack of integrity coming from the scientific community isn't just limited to the Miller Experiment. Now, let's continue on our journey…

A Magnified Problem

If the lack of integrity from the Miller Experiment wasn't enough already, let's land this plane down on the runway as we take a look at the compounded problem of cell formation. For the sake of argument, let's go ahead and use what Miller was able to manufacture [*by means of his intelligence*] to see if he answered the question of HOW life came to be on planet earth. As stated earlier, the first step in creating life is to create a usable amino acid. Miller's experiment yielded an extremely small amount of usable amino acids, and a lot of garbage. As a matter of fact, after hundreds of replications and modifications using techniques similar to the Miller Experiment, scientists have only been able to produce very small amounts of less than half of the 20 amino acids required for life. The rest require much more complex fusion conditions. Again, for the sake of argument, let's be fair to our investigation and say that hypothetically Miller was able to create all 20 amino acids necessary for life to *only* begin. What is the next step in the formation of a cell-life? Let's start with a simple illustration, and then unpack what that means:

DNA → RNA → AMINO ACIDS → PROTIENS → SINGLE CELL → DNA

If the first step for cell creation is amino acids, why does the above diagram start with DNA? I'm glad you asked. Follow with me for a moment as we unpack cell formation. Trust me – you'll be blown away by the logic for this one!

I used to think that left-handed people were simply weird. I mean, most of them position the paper sideways as they write… what's up with that? It wasn't until I started studying Abiogenesis (*the origin of life from nonliving matter*) that I realized something profound; **ALL** life is made up of **ONLY** Left-Handed amino acids! Every amino acid has an identical [Right-Handed] match in a mirror image. Just like how when you put your hands together like you are praying the old-fashioned way, they fit perfectly together. But when you pull them apart, they are complete opposites. So is the same with amino acids. There are left and right-handed amino acids in existence. However, **EVERY** living thing is comprised of only left-handed amino acids. Several complex amino acids are then joined together to form a string of dozens of amino acids. If even a single right-handed amino acid were to attempt to join the string, the entire string would be rendered useless. The exactness of the amino string is extremely critical in the proceeding process of forming a single protein molecule. Amino acids string together and are bent and wound into the perfect shape that [becomes] forms a single protein. There are over 1500 different proteins in one single cell of a human being. Then, like amino acids, proteins are perfectly strung together to create a single cell.

Wrap Your Mind Around This

First, you have to create at least 20 left-handed *only* amino acids. Then, you have to perfectly arrange their string and bending sequence to create one single protein molecule. This process has to happen over 1500 different times, in different ways, involving different sequences of amino acids perfectly strung together in order to form the over 1500 necessary proteins. Finally, you have to perfectly string over 1500 proteins together to form a single cell. Keep in mind, that with all the scientific advancements we have been able to make like sending man to the moon, cloning animals, putting a rover on mars, etc.… scientists have yet to come close to the very first piece of the cell puzzle. Now compound that with what needs to take place if you could even produce the amino acids in the first place. It's no wonder that Francis Crick, the Nobel Prize winner for the co-discovery of the double-helix shape of DNA, said the following, *"An honest man, armed with all the knowledge available to us now, could only state that in some sense, the origin of life appears at the moment to be almost a miracle, so many are the conditions which would have had to have been satisfied to get it going."*[xi] Unfortunately, even though he understood that life's origins were nothing short of miraculous, Crick died an atheist. Crick's legacy is that he was part of a duo that discovered the complexity of DNA.

Which Came First – The Chicken or the Egg?

Before we unpack how DNA and cell creation works, I'd like to share something super profound and yet, super simple with you. Scientists from Sheffield and Warwick universities found that the formation of an egg's shell relies on a protein found only in a chicken's ovaries. Therefore, an egg can only exist if it has been inside a chicken. The protein - called ovocledidin-17, or OC-17 - acts as a catalyst to speed up the development of the shell. This hard shell is essential to house the yolk and its protective fluids while the chick develops inside.[xii] This settles once and for all the question about whether the chicken came before the egg. Seems like common sense, but this fact has been disputed for centuries! According to modern science, you have to have a fully developed chicken in order to have an egg. This truth matches the account of creation on Day Six of the Biblical account found in the book of Genesis.

So, how do amino acids know how to arrange themselves into complex strings that bend into perfectly formed proteins? I'm glad you asked [you ask great questions. You're a fart smeller, I mean smart fellar!]. This is quite frankly one of the biggest problems faced by modern evolutionary scientists. Thanks to advancements in micro-science we now know with great certainty how amino acids form. Inside the center of a cell is the cell nucleus – the brain of the cell. Outside of the nucleus, contained within the walls of the cell membrane is cytoplasm. Amino acids live inside the cytoplasm. Inside of the nucleus is where DNA lives. **D**eoxyribo**N**ucleic **A**cid is a molecule that carries the genetic instructions used in growth, development, functioning, and reproduction of all known living organisms. DNA is comprised of four nucleotides [**C**ytosine – **G**uanine – **A**denine – **T**hymine] These four nucleotides are strung together in base pairs and held by a twisted double-helix ladder-type sugar-phosphate backbone. DNA tells everything where to go and what to do when it gets there. DNA tells our bodies how tall we are, what color hair or eyes that we have, etc. Without DNA, molecules are lost wanderers without any direction for what they are supposed to do.

Inside the nucleus of the cell, DNA makes short copies of parts of its string sequence called RNA. **R**ibo**N**ucleic **A**cid is short enough to pass through a port in the wall of the nucleus and travel into the cytoplasm inside the cell. Once RNA is in the cytoplasm, a molecular machine called a Ribosome extracts the exact amino acids that are living in the cytoplasm and forms them into string sequences that form proteins. This process is continuously repeated ultimately causing a new cell to be created. So, DNA is required to tell which amino acids are to go into the ribosome from the cytoplasm in order to correctly form a protein, which creates a cell, which is where DNA lives.

Wait a Minute!

If DNA has to exist in a cell in order for amino acids to know how to assemble, that means the cell has to exist before a cell can be created, which is rule number three in Cell Biology – *"All cells come from pre-existing cells through reproduction."* How then can an evolutionist claim that a pre-biotic soup can assemble random amino acids to form life without instructions from DNA? It doesn't take a rocket scientist to establish that this is a logical fallacy. It seems science has confirmed that in order to make a cell, you have to first have a completed cell to start with, just like the fact that you have to have a completed chicken in order to lay an egg.

What we have discovered here is that the special creation of a complete cell from the very beginning is the best explanation from what our evidences provide. After the sixth day of creation, God rested because, *"the heavens and the earth were finished, and all the host of them."* (Genesis 2:1)

DNA is a Complex Library of Information

In a recent documentary, Ray Comfort hit the streets to ask self-proclaimed evolutionists if a book could create itself. Comfort handed each person a book and asked them if colors could randomly fall out of the sky to produce the vibrant pictures that were scattered throughout the hundreds of pages in the book. Then he asked them if black ink could randomly place itself around the pictures in coherent forms of words, sentences, and paragraphs. Obviously, there wasn't a single person who said that they believed that the book could randomly create itself. It would be intellectual suicide to believe that even if billions of years of chance were available, a book cannot and will not ever randomly form. A book can't create itself – it needs an author who can arrange colors into beautiful pictures and systematically order the letter sequences to give them valuable meanings.

Do these 24 letters make any sense to you:
"shsoTeienhmgnnectianesan."

You're probably thinking, "What are you talking about?" The letters in that scrambled sentence are present, yes. However, they have no organization to make them have any meaning at all. It takes intelligence to arrange those same 24 letters to form a cohesive sentence. If I use my brainpower, I can arrange those 24 letters to spell out: *"This sentence makes no sense."* Letters by themselves have no meaning. Even if letters could randomly appear in that book, it would take an intelligent mind to organize the sequence of letters for them to make a coherent sentence. After Comfort got the evolutionists to agree that a book could not create itself, he asked them a simple question – *"Could DNA create itself?"*

DNA is an incredibly complex language that encodes all genetic information for all living things. DNA organizes its letters (*Nucleotides*) into words (*Codons*) that form sentences (*Genes*) which makes paragraphs (*Chromosomes*) eventually making a full novel (*Genomes*). The DNA in your cells is bundled into 46 chromosomes in the nucleus of the cell. There are 3 Billion base pairs in each cell that fit into a space just 6 microns across. Six microns is so tiny that you would need scanning, tunneling, and atomic force microscope to even see that (no, you can't buy one of those on Amazon). Even with this advanced technology, DNA only looks as if it is a string rather than being viewable down to its distinct parts from which it is made up of. If you were to stretch the DNA from just **ONE** single cell in your body, it would be over six and a half feet long. If you strung the entire DNA in your body together, it would be about twice the diameter of the Solar System!

A single gram of DNA holds up to 700 terabytes of specifically coded information. There are over 200 grams of DNA in your body. If you were to attempt to store all the information from your DNA onto the densest storage device designed to date, you would need over 46,000 – 3 Terabyte hard drives to accomplish that. It is said that Google processes about 25 petabytes of information per day. Unbelievably, you could store the entirety of what Google processes in a day into less than 5 grams of DNA. Think of it this way - all the written works of mankind created since the beginning of recorded history in all languages equals about 50 petabytes of information, which could be stored on a mere 10 grams of your DNA. Your DNA could store everything ever written and still have 190 grams left for more storage!

| P a g e

Now tell me this – If a simple 200-page book could not logically create itself, then how in the world could a 140,000 Terabyte information system create itself? DNA reeks of extraordinary special creation when compared to what ordinary man has accomplished in all his time on earth.

> **Reader's Note:**
> Ok, stretch! Take a breath. We're going to land this scientific plane here shortly. If you're already convinced God HAS TO exist as an explanation for HOW We Got Here, then flip to the end of this chapter. But, for those who still aren't convinced, read on for facts that should solidify any doubts you may still have. Trust me, it took a LOT of facts for me, which is why I'm beating up these points for you.

Irreducibly Complex City Inside the Cell

Looking through a high-powered electron microscope, you will see a city full of complex infrastructure inside each and every cell in your body. The Cell Membrane looks like a brick city wall constructed by lipids. The Cytoskeleton provides routes for transportation from one end of the cell to the other. Mitochondria are the energy plants that produce energy by converting fuel into useable cellular energy. Lysosomes are the recycling plant that takes worn-out waste inside the cell and reuses it into different nutrients to fuel the cell. The Nucleus is the city's library system where DNA is stored. Ribosomes are at work building new cells from RNA copies.

City Walls, Transportation Services, Energy Plants, Recycling Plants, Library Systems, Replication Factories, etc. All confined to a very, very extremely small space that it is invisible to the naked eye. Here's the thing though, if one part were removed from the inner workings of the cell, the cell could not function properly, and therefore would be useless. This is a premise known as *"Irreducible*

Complexity," which suggests that every working part contained within an organism must appear <u>fully</u> functional <u>together,</u> <u>all</u> at the <u>same</u> exact <u>time</u>. If one simple part were to be removed, the entire organism would fail. Every part is dependent on the other in order for the whole to work at all.

Michael Behe coined the example of a simple rat trap with all its working parts as an easy way to understand Irreducible Complexity. A rat trap starts with a wooden base, a hammer wire that traps the rat, a hold-down bar that connects to the bait tray when set, and multiple staples that hold all of these to the wood base. Now, suppose you remove any single one of those parts, would the trap still function? No, it would not. Even if you removed the simplest single staple that holds the bait tray, you wouldn't be able to set the trap. If there were no bait tray, where would the cheese go? If the wood base weren't there, nothing could connect. Simple logic shows us that the entire rat trap would have to be assembled by skilled hands all at the same exact time in order to function. Remove one part = no functionality!

Now, apply this same simple logic to the cell. If the lysosomes weren't in the cell, waste would build up and the toxicity would kill the cell. If there weren't any mitochondria, how would the cell be energized to live? Remove DNA and you have a bunch of lost parts with no direction. Without the cell wall, the whole cell would just explode everywhere. The ENTIRE cell has to be present for the cell to function properly. Remove one single element of the city, and the city collapses. The city inside a cell is irreducibly complex.

The reason why this is so vitally important is because the truth of irreducible complexity completely flies in the face of what evolution depends on to be true. Natural Selection depends on extremely small mutations that constantly occur over a very extensively long period of time in order for anything to develop at all. By evolutionary methods, the ribosome would have to be one of many trial and errors. But why would a ribosome exist if there were no

DNA to feed it RNA? And how could it be energized to replicate if the energy created by mitochondria came years later?

Consider this – the human eye requires the retina, cornea, iris, pupil, lens, muscles, etc. to all function together simultaneously. Heck just remove the lens and the iris, cornea, and pupil would be completely exposed and dry out from contact with air. Remove one simple muscle and the whole eye would just flop around aimlessly. Even if you had a fully functioning eye, without a fully functioning brain, there would be nothing to interpret the upside-down signals that are being sent. Remove one single element to the eye and it stops working. It is as irreducibly complex as the lungs, blood-clotting, hearing, and the cell, etc.

Mr. Darwin had this to say about the evolution of organisms… *"If it could be demonstrated that any complex organ existed, which could not possibly have been formed by numerous, successive, slight modifications, my theory would absolutely break down. But I can find out no such case."*[xiii] I hate to tell you Mr. Darwin, but we just demonstrated a small portion of what our modern science has to tell us about the impossibility of organs developing at extremely slow paces by numerous, successive, slight modifications. Your theory just broke down!

"Come now, and let us reason together, says the Lord."

In the 18th verse of the very first chapter of Isaiah's prophecies, the Lord tells Isaiah that they should join together and apply proper reasoning to Israel's state of affairs in order that the people would know for certain what the proper understanding of their situations were. Vigilant reasoning is the key to knowing what truth is, or what is false. Reasoning is the one of the many evidences that separates man from the rest of God's creation. We are His crowning glory[xiv], created in His image[xv], and have the ability to ponder our own existence, unlike any other creature that God created.

The apostle Paul knew the importance of reasoning when it came to his public ministry. It is my belief that Paul would've preferred to have only ever talked about him meeting the resurrected Christ, for he said, *"I decided to know nothing among you except Jesus Christ and him crucified."*[xvi] However, he understood that because we were created in God's image, there are many who would need more logical evidence to support the belief in the risen Messiah that Paul was so excited to talk about. For this reason, Paul *"became all things to all people, that by all means I might save some."*[xvii] It is well-documented that Paul *"reasoned in the synagogue with both Jews and God-fearing Greeks, as well as in the marketplace day by day with those who happened to be there."*[xviii] Paul's example is one that we should follow as we seek to answer the deep questions that we face in life.

We are created to be logical, rational people who use sound reasoning to determine what the truth is about how we got here on planet earth. There are three forms of reasoning that we will use to examine the scientific facts we have already studied. The first, and most popular form of reasoning is called, *"Deductive Reasoning."* Deductive reasoning is a basic form of valid reasoning that starts with a general statement (hypothesis), and examines the probabilities to reach a specific, logical conclusion. In deductive reasoning, if something is true of a class of things in general, it is also true for all members of that class. For example:
A) All men are mortal.
  B) Harold is a man.
    C) Therefore, Harold is mortal.

For deductive reasoning to be sound, the hypothesis must be correct. It is assumed that the premises, "All men are mortal" and "Harold is a man" are true. Therefore, the conclusion is logical and true. Now, let's take what we have already learned about cell creation (our tested hypothesis), and apply sound deductive reasoning to it, to determine what the true evidences point to about our existence.

A) All cells have to be created.
  B) All cells need an existing complete cell in order to be created.
    C) Therefore, a completed cell had to exist before a cell can be created.

So, using deductive reasoning, we can clearly see the answer to the question of our origins becomes quite easy to answer. However, to be fair and honest in our adventures, let's look at a second method of applying reason to our research.

"Inductive Reasoning" is a method of compiling all of the available information, and then formulate a conclusion based on the strong evidences that supports the premise. Unlike deductive reasoning, whose conclusion is very certain, the truth of the conclusion of an inductive argument is probable, based upon the evidence given. Let's recap the evidences we have already covered and see where the natural conclusion leads us to believe.

1) We started by examining the claims from what is called, "Cell Theory." Cell Theory states that all living things are composed of one or more cells, which are the basic life structure of a living thing or organism, and that all cells come from pre-existing cells through reproduction.

2) Next, we compared chemical evolution to baking a cake. We saw the utter impossibility for chemical evolution to ever explain how a single usable amino acid could be created by itself. We learned that the Miller/Urey experiment cheated with a priori knowledge (they already had grandma's cake recipe – but remember that there is no guide to chemical evolution) to support their experiment's chances for a successful outcome. They also knew that oxygen would destroy the amino acids that they did manage to create, so they used their own physical efforts to intelligently remove the acids before they were destroyed.

3) My favorite part of our journey was when we looked at the chicken or egg comparison to DNA creation. Similar to Cell Theory, DNA is necessary to create RNA, which is where the replication process takes place. You have to have a fully functioning and completed chicken (DNA) to produce an egg (RNA).

4) To further fascinate us, we learned that DNA is by far the most intense storage facility that has ever been invented. All the written works of mankind created since the beginning of recorded history in all languages equals about 50 petabytes of information, which could be stored on a mere 10 grams of your DNA. Your DNA could store everything ever written and still have 190 grams left for more storage!

5) The fact that a single-cell is *"Irreducibly Complex"* provides us with the security that again, a fully-functioning, complete cell must exist for life to exist at all. If we removed even a single component to a cell's operation system, the cell would fail and die. The city inside the cell must all exist, all at the same time, in order to function.

Let's simplify our five facts into a smaller set of information in order for us to apply the Inductive Reasoning process to our investigation:

1) Life requires life to exist.
2) Cakes and Amino Acids cannot blindly create themselves.
3) You cannot have DNA replication without a fully functioning cell.
4) DNA is unimaginably complex in terms of information storage capabilities.
5) A fully functioning city inside a cell is irreducibly complex.

If I were to undertake providing all of the great evidences for our origins in this book, it would be too large for most to want to read. However, if we look at just these five simple facts about our beginnings, our conclusion becomes ever clearer. The most logical premise that can be supported by our five simple facts is that there must be a Creator who gave life to every complex organism on earth.

Furthermore, the overwhelming complexity of cell creation and intelligence contained within DNA and cells should make us stand in awe of our Creator. The obvious common theme is that something has to exist *first* in order for anything to exist at all. Something had to precede the beginning of the universe for life to exist. Without going into great details for a really excellent argument, I want to sum up our inductive reasoning conclusion by examining what's known as the Kalam Cosmological Argument. The argument uses deductive reasoning to come to its natural conclusion.

A) Anything that *begins* to exist must have a cause.
   B) The Universe (Life) began to exist.
      C) The Universe (Life) must have a cause.

This leads us to our final examination of reasoning called, "*Abductive Reasoning.*" Abductive reasoning seeks to look at all the theories that exist, and make its conclusion based on the "*Inference to the Best Explanation.*" Now, remember we started off by stating that there are really only two options out there that attempt to explain the origins of our existence. Either Evolution can make a valid claim to support the known scientific evidences, or Special Creation is the best answer. It is important to state that both of these theories can be completely wrong, but it is impossible for both to be right; both cannot be mutually true, given that they are both wholly opposed to one another.

To recap, the theory of evolution claims that there is nothing behind our origins. That nothing exists except for the natural. Evolution uses natural selection to choose the best mutations that occur, but it must be specified that these mutations originally occur by the following means:
1) The process is blind.

2) The process is merely accidental.
3) The process is wholly unguided.
4) The process is completely unintelligent.

I'm reminded what Forrest Gump once said when talking to Jenny. He said, *"I'm not a smart man, but I know what love is."* Let me paraphrase this for our own journey today… *"We may not all be molecular biologists, but I know what intelligent design looks like!"* Using the scientific evidences available to us it is quite obvious that there is absolutely nothing blind, accidental, or unguided about the process of creating life. On the contrary, you have to have a Designer, an Artist, a creative Mind, an all-seeing, all-knowing God who preceded the first moment of life. Given the overwhelming evidences available to all of us, the inference to the best explanation is that Special Creation is the culprit behind our origins.

"For what can be known about God is plain to them because God has shown it to them. For his invisible attributes, namely, his eternal power and divine nature, have been clearly perceived, ever since the creation of the world, in the things that have been made. So, they are without excuse."[xix]

You Are Specially Created!

I've got some really good news for you… *"God created man in his own image, in the image of God he created him; male and female he created them."*[xx] You are unlike every other creature that God made. Think about it, have you ever seen a monkey ponder their own existence? You may say, how would we know what a monkey is thinking? But alas, you just discovered the true meaning of your differences! You can talk, ask questions, think, plan, learn, explore, build, discover, and appreciate your surroundings. Man has traveled to the moon and back looking for answers. We've built thousands of schools and universities to educate ourselves. We've developed computers that can process massive amounts of information to aide us in things like medical advancements that extend our time here on earth. Now, when's the last time you've seen a monkey, or ANY other creature do anything like that? We're not simply different, we are **extremely** different from every other known creature under the sun. Amen!

I'm going rearrange the order of this book a bit, because I want to save the "Why" portion of this book for later. It's my favorite!!!

WHERE
Do We Go When We Die?

If the most logical outcome of my investigations into the meaning of life led me to believe that once we die, we are merely put into the ground and eaten by worms, than that is the worldview I would claim. However, if there is ample evidence for life after death, then it would do us well to do some research on what happens next…

ARE we more than just a physical property?

As we covered in the last chapter, evolutionists hole to a position where everything is merely physical in nature, and metaphysics cannot exist. When I was an atheist, I held the views of a physicalist. Physicalism is a philosophical position holding that everything which exists is no more extensive than its physical properties; that is, that there are no kinds of things other than physical things.[xxi] I did not believe or allow for anything "*supernatural*" [metaphysical]. That is, anything beyond what is natural; unexplainable by natural law or phenomena; especially when it would pertain to the nature attributed to God. But, as you read in my opening testimony, what happened to me that night was something so beyond natural that I had no choice to swallow my pride and admit that maybe I needed to look more into this physicalist view that I had held onto so dearly for all of my life. If everything was purely physical in nature, then we should be able to study the natural patterns of "*things*" and deduce how these "*things*" should behave in any given situation since there are no other agents at work behind the scenes like a mind to make decisions about things.

Take a cloud for example. A cloud is the purely physical property of liquid water droplets or solid ice crystals that form into visible clouds. Wind is also the purely natural movement of air of any velocity. We can study the effects of wind and clouds and make predictions about their behavior because they are both purely natural properties. If the wind blows from the east, which direction will it push the cloud along? If you said west, you are a scientist. (You wouldn't believe the answers I've heard through the years of asking that same question to a live audience ☺) If the wind blows from the south, we can accurately predict that the cloud will be pushed to the north; that is if there are no tornadoes around. You see, because we are dealing with purely physical/natural processes, we can scientifically predict how these properties should behave.

Now, if we use the same naturalistic logic when applied to human beings, could we predict the same type of outcomes as we did with the purely physical cloud? What would a human being do if they were to be dropped into a pool of water with man-eating sharks?

Person A) Freaks out and screams for their mama!
Person B) Attempts to befriend and pet the sharks.
Person C) Passes out and gets eaten by sharks.
Person D) Punches sharks in the nose and owns them.
Person E) Rides them like a dolphin at SeaWorld.
Person F) I don't know, I'm out of cool ideas ☺

Let's be honest, Persons A and C are most likely going to be the case, but can we really know for sure? I've seen some crazy footage of people who actually live like Persons D and E. And if it were a dog instead of a shark, Person B would be my daughter-in-law, Alyssa, who can't not pet a dog. I don't care if the thing is foaming at the mouth and growling like a roaring lion, she is going to try and pet that dog. She really needs an intervention or something. I, on the other hand, don't even like being around certain breeds of dogs, even though I'm a total dog person. Alyssa and I are totally different about that. Wait; did you see what just happened there? Alyssa and I would have different outcomes because we are different people. Oh yah, sharks! (I told you I had A.D.D.) None of us could actually accurately predict what any of said persons in the pool of sharks would do because each person is so different from one another. There's something beyond the physical nature of people that causes them to think or rationalize differently than others. Unlike the clouds that have no mental capacity, human beings do have thoughts that are private to them and determine outcomes.

We ARE MORE than just a physical property!

"It seems to me immensely unlikely that the mind is a mere by-product of matter. For if my mental processes are determined wholly by the motions of atoms in my brain, I have no reason to suppose that my beliefs are true. They may be sound chemically, but that does not make them sound logically. And hence I have no reason for supposing my brain to be composed of atoms."[xxii]

What makes human behavior unpredictable is that in addition to the Body (*physical being*), we also have a nonphysical component called a "*Soul, Mind*," or "*Self*." This reality that we are more than just a physical body is what's known as "*Substance Dualism*." It is actually quite easy to see this nature about us.

Take dreams for example. Dreams are incredible experiences that we have when we are in an unconscious state of sleep. Dreams are very personal and cannot be shared. This is because dreams can only exist in the separate part of our being that we call our minds. There has never been a time when a husband and wife were sleeping next to each other and woke up to compare the same dream with one another. Even though they were physically in the same place, their consciences were completely separated within themselves. Scientists can hook up probes that can determine how often a person dreams and how intense the R.E.M. (Rapid Eye Movement) dreams are because those observable signs are coming from the physical part of the person being studied. However, in order for the scientist to "*know*" what the content of the person's dream is about, they would have to wake the patient up and ask them to describe their dreams, because that part is located in the mind of the patient.

One of the most fascinating studies I've come across was from a world-renowned neuroscientist named Wilder Penfield. Penfield operated on over a thousand epilepsy patients while they were awake (under local anesthesia), and he stimulated their physical brains with electrodes in order to identify epileptic regions for surgical resection. He carefully recorded their responses to stimulation in his book, *"Mystery of the Mind."* What Penfield discovered while doing his research gave tremendous insight into how the human mind and physical brain work separately from one another.

> *"When I have caused a conscious patient to move his hand by applying an electrode to the motor cortex of one hemisphere, I have often asked him about it. Invariably his response was: "I didn't do that. You did". When I caused him to vocalize, he said: "I didn't make that sound. You pulled it out of me."*[xxiii]

Penfield never encountered a patient who, with stimulation of the brain, thought that he (the patient) had willed it. The patient could always distinguish between acts he willed himself and acts imposed on him by the surgeon's electrode. In every case the patient thought of themselves as having a separate *"Self"* apart from their physical bodies. Interestingly, no matter where the Cerebral Cortex was probed, there was no place that Penfield could make a patient *"think"* or *"believe"* something. Again, this is because apart from the body, we have a soul, mind, or self.

The Bible often addresses this reality as well.

> **"And he answered, 'You shall love the Lord your God with all your heart and with all your soul and with all your strength and with your entire MIND.'"**[xxiv]

> **"Do not be conformed to this world, but be transformed by the renewal of your MIND, that by testing you may discern what is the will of God, what is good and acceptable and perfect."**[xxv]

> **"For to set the MIND on the flesh is death, but to set the MIND on the Spirit is life and peace."**[xxvi]

> *"Set your MINDS on things that are above,*
> *not on things that are on earth."*[xxvii]

The bible makes it clear that we have been given a mind to use, and it would do us well to use it properly.

A.D.D. Alert – Side Note 1

God gave us a mind in order that we can use it to make decisions. If He wanted robots, He would've created us without a mind to think and rationalize to make choices. God purposely made us with the ability to choose things, like whether we choose to receive His love, and in return, love Him back. God is a gentleman; He never forces Himself on anyone. His whole desire is that we use our minds to choose to love Him. Those choices that we are given is referred to as our *"free will."* God gave us the freedom to choose good or bad, right or wrong, light or darkness, love or hate, etc. Now, in creating us with free will, He also created us with the capacity to choose what is opposed (evil) to His perfect nature (good). I've often heard it said, "If God were a good God, why doesn't He stop evil from happening?" While on the surface that seems like a reasonable question, the answer is quite simple yet a profound explanation of the world we see around us.

Let's suppose God stops a person from raping another person. We would naturally think that God was awesome for doing so. However, what if He didn't stop the next person that was going to do the same to another? Wouldn't He have to stop that one as well? What about the murderer? What about the thief? If He stops one, wouldn't He have to stop them all? And if He stops them all, where does that end? Liars, adulterers, back-stabbers, blasphemers, etc. Where does His intervention end? If God intervened on every bad decision that we humans make, He would have to intervene on everything all the time, and that would mean that He violated our free will, and therefore we are back to the robots who have no ability to think or rationalize on our life decisions.

The reality is that God will not stop you, or anyone else, from using your freewill. He can't, or else He created it for no reason. God desires for us to seek Him in all of our decisions. If we did that, we would never commit heinous acts of violence against one another. We wouldn't lie and cheat one another. No, we would seek to be a blessing to those around us. Think about a world where everyone used their freewill to choose God's plan and purpose for living. Wow, what a place that would be. Wait, that place is coming soon; will you be a part of it? Wait, I'm getting ahead of myself; back to trying to convince you that there's life after death.

<u>The Table vs. The Human Body</u>

My wife loves our old coffee table. One day, one of the legs on the coffee table broke off by accident, so I went to the hardware store to buy a replacement. The color was pretty close, but the style of the leg was totally different. Being a man, I figured that would be acceptable; Not! My wife wasn't satisfied with that. She actually liked the new leg better than the old, so I bought three more legs just like the new one and put them on that old table. Well, I wish that were the end of the story, but it's not. Those four new legs were really shiny because they were brand new. They made the top of the old table look worn out now, so she requested a new top to match the shininess of the new legs. So, like any good husband, I went back to the store and bought a shiny new top for that old table. Now, she was a happy wife – Happy Wife = Happy Life!

The table never left the room it was in while I worked on it. At one point, it had mixed parts. One by one I threw away the old pieces once I replaced them with new. So, is the table a different table than the original, or is it the same old table that has always been there?

[...getting another cup of coffee while you think about that one... don't overthink it]

If you said different, you are correct! The old table was totally replaced and thrown away. What is left in its place is a brand-new physical table. The table physically renewed and became a totally different table. Now here's the thing, according to Stanford School of Medicine's Institute for Stem Cell Biology and Regenerative Medicine, *"Every one of us completely regenerates our own skin every 7 days... Every single cell in our skeleton is replaced every 7 years. The future of medicine lies in understanding how the body creates itself out of a single cell and the mechanisms by which it renews itself throughout life."*

That's right, every 7 years, you are physically a new you! Assuming the same about the table is also true for you, you're going to have to apply for a new social security number, name, driver's license, etc. I mean, you are a totally different person, just like the table, right? I'm being silly. Of course you're not going to have to apply for a new identity every 7 years, because unlike the table, you are more than just a physical bag of cells. You have a glue that holds you together throughout the different physical bodies you have during your life, and that glue is called your soul. I am on my 7th body by now, but I'm still the same old Dave that I've been since my mom gave birth to me and the government assigned me a number. It would be ludicrous if every 7 years a person renamed themselves because technically, they are a different physical body. By comparing the table with the human body, we can easily see that there is something that goes beyond our physical being that makes us different from purely natural explanations for why we are the way we are.

A.D.D. Alert – Side Note 2

We are technically a "triune" being. We have a physical body, a soul, AND we have the ability to possess a Spirit. I say ability because some of us will choose to never accept that Spirit to come and live inside of us and complete us. We are born with a dead spirit, but through Christ we can be made alive in the Spirit and be completed as we always were meant to be – but more on that later.

I do want to touch on this interesting little tidbit of information, though. We, HUMANS, have a body, soul, and spirit. We are TOTALLY different from anything else that God created. We are the ONLY one's able to possess a Spirit, unlike the plant and animal kingdoms.

Plants are only physical things that have life because they are plugged into physical nature. They draw water, air, and sun into themselves, but they have no animation to them whatsoever because they do not possess a soul. Animals have physical bodies and souls that give them animation. Even an ant has a soul because it has the ability to move and perform instinctual tasks. However, no insect or animal is capable of possessing a spirit; that is something uniquely special and available to humans alone. So, the next time someone tries to call you an evolved animal, just let them know that you have a spirit (or at least the ability to have one), which knocks you out of the running.

<u>NDE</u> – <u>Near Death Experiences</u>

Approximately 8 million people living in America have experienced what's known as a Near Death Experience (we will call them NDE's from here on out; I'll blame the short cut on my carpal tunnel). It is not uncommon for people who experience an NDE to claim things like hearing themselves being pronounced dead, undergoing some type of out-of-body event, encountering a bright light, traveling through a tunnel, hearing beautiful music, etc. Commonalities like these claims is what began to intrigue me about NDE's, but it was important to me that I would be able to validate their experiences in some way. I didn't just want to *"take their word for it,"* you know what I mean? It's cool that someone says, *"they saw grandpa, and he looked amazing at 30 years old,"* or that, *"Aunt Jane is beautiful once again and is singing like she used to."* Don't get me wrong, those sentiments are awesome, and may be true, but we have no way of confirming said reports. It's completely possible that the people just experienced a really intense dream or something. I needed more than that for me to feel like I could bank on there truly being evidence for life beyond the physical body. I needed to see things that would be impossible for the patient to know about yet be able to give exact details about things they were able to see, hear, and experience while being clinically dead.

What Do You Mean, I'm Dead?

What does it mean to physically die? There are two components that doctors look at to determine that someone can be officially pronounced "*dead.*" First, patients need to be "*Heart-Dead.*" An electrocardiogram — abbreviated as EKG or ECG — is a test that measures the electrical activity of the heartbeat. With each beat, an electrical impulse (or "*wave*") travels through the heart. This wave causes the muscle to squeeze and pump blood from the heart.[xxviii] When a person physically dies, their heart stops beating, therefore no electrical impulse is generated. At this stage, the patient is now heart dead. The second event that takes place is called "*Brain-Death.*" Within 11–20 seconds of the heart stopping, the brain ceases to receive the oxygen necessary to continue functioning, thus causing brain death. A patient determined to be brain dead is legally and clinically dead.[xxix] The following examples have all met this criterion for actually being physically dead. So, as we venture through just a few testimonies (I know of hundreds, but this book is supposed to be short), keep in the back of your mind that if we are only physical beings, as evolutionary theory supposes, then what explanation could be had that would best explain [remember: "*inference to the best explanation*" on page 46] how these people are able to give such exact details about the circumstances they experienced?

What Do You Mean By That?

We are going to look at cases where clinically dead people give details that are:

A) Evidential: relating to; or based on evidence
B) Veridical: corresponding to facts; not illusory; real

Example Testimony:
An experiment was conducted by Dr. Lawrence at Hartford Hospital in Connecticut, in 1994, when she was Director of Nursing Education and Research there. She placed a scrolling LED display high on a cabinet in the room [of the electrophysiology lab], not visible to anyone standing on the floor. In order to read the sign a person needed to use a ladder or some other type of vessel that could take them high enough to see the sign at all. She randomly changed the message displayed on the sign to sayings that made no sense at all so that no one could say they overheard a conversation about the words on the sign.

During one of Dr. Lawrence's surgery, her patients heart stopped beating (heart-dead) for over 10 minutes (brain-dead). She worked hard to resuscitate the patient, and eventually succeeded. When the patient awoke, they explained to the doctors about having some sort of out-of-body experience where they felt like they were floating above their bodies in the surgical room, and seeing a weird sign that said, *"Popsicles are in bloom."* Excitedly, Dr. Lawrence said, *"You are the first patient who has ever read that sign. That sign can only be read by someone reading it from the vantage point of the ceiling. And because you were able to read this sign and tell us about it, you have proven scientifically that the mind can function outside of the brain and body."*[xxx]

This is an example of information that could not have been known to the patient, yet clearly evidenced as observable information that can be tested and verified.

Cases That Make You Go Hmmm…

Case #1: Dr. Kim Clark

Maria was a migrant worker who had a severe heart attack while visiting friends in Seattle. She was rushed to Harborview Hospital and placed in the coronary care unit. A few days later, she had a cardiac arrest but was fortunately resuscitated. The following day, Dr. Kim Clark, who was the doctor that resuscitated her, paid her a visit. Maria told Clark that during her cardiac arrest she was able to look down from the ceiling and watch the medical team at work on her body. At one point in this experience, Maria said she found herself outside the hospital and spotted a tennis shoe on the ledge of the north side of the third floor of the building. She was able to provide several details regarding its appearance, including the observations that one of its laces was stuck underneath the heel and that the little toe area was worn. Maria wanted to know for sure whether she had *"really"* seen that shoe, and she begged Clark to try to locate it.

Quite skeptical, Clark went to the location described by Maria—and found the tennis shoe. From the window of her hospital room, the details that Maria had recounted could not be discerned. But upon retrieval of the shoe, Clark confirmed Maria's observations. Clark concluded, *"The only way she could have had such a perspective, was if she had been floating right outside and at very close range to the tennis shoe. I retrieved the shoe and brought it back to Maria; it was very concrete evidence for me."*[xxxi]

Case #2: Dr. Lloyd Rudy & Dr. Roberto Cattaneo
Actual Transcript of Dr. Rudy's Experience:[xxxii]
"We had a very unfortunate individual who on Christmas Day had, from an oral infection, infected his heart valve. Along with one of my junior partners that was on call, we had to do an emergency valve resection. Once we were able to accomplish the repair of the aneurysm and the replacement of the valve, we could not get the person off of the bypass. Every time the four or five liters of blood

that we were pumping around his body, we would reduce down to two or three, he'd begin to weaken, and his blood pressure would go down, and so on. To make a long story short: We simply couldn't get him off the heart-lung machine. Finally, we just had to give up. I mean, we said: We cannot get him off of the heart-lung machine, so we're going to have to pronounce him dead. Nobody bothered to turn off the machine that records blood pressure, and the pulse of the man.

Well, the assistant surgeon and I went in and took our gowns off, and gloves, and masks, and things, and came back, and we were in our short-sleeve shirts, and we were standing at the door, kind of discussing if there was anything else we could have done and any other medicines we could have given, whatever, to have made this a success. And as we were standing there, it had been at least 20 minutes. I don't know this exact time sequence, but it was close to 20–25 minutes, that this man recorded no heartbeat, no blood pressure, and the echo showing no movement of the heart, just sitting.

And all of a sudden, we looked up, and we saw some electrical activity. And pretty soon, the electrical activity turned into a heartbeat. Very slow, 30, 40-a-minute, and we thought, "Well, that's kind of an agonal thing," and we see that, occasionally, that the heart will continue to beat even though the patient can't generate a blood pressure or pump any blood. Well, pretty soon we look, and he's actually generating a pressure. Now, we are not doing anything; I mean, the machines are all shut off. And we'd stopped all the medicines, and all that.

So, I started yelling, "Get anesthesia back in here!" and, "Get the nurses!" To make a very long story short, without putting him back on cardiopulmonary bypass or heart-lung machine and stuff, we started giving him some medicines, and anesthesia started giving him oxygen. And pretty soon he had a blood pressure of 80, and pretty soon a blood pressure of 100, and his heart rate was now up to a 100 a minute. He recovered and had no neurologic deficit. And for the next 10 days [to] two weeks, all of us went in and were talking to him about what he experienced, if anything. And he talked about the bright light at the end of the tunnel, as I recall, and so on. But the thing that astounded me was that he described that operating room floating around and saying, "I saw you and Dr. Cattaneo standing in the doorway with your arms folded, talking. I didn't know where the anesthesiologist was, but he came running back in. And I saw all of these Post-its [Post-it notes] sitting on this TV screen," he said.

And what those [Post-it notes] were, was where any call I [Dr. Rudy] got, the nurse would write down who called and the phone number and stick it on the monitor, and then the next Post-it would stick to that Post-it, and then I'd have a string of Post-its of phone calls I had to make. He described that! I mean, there is no way he could have described that before the operation, because I didn't have any calls, right?

He was up there. He described the scene, things that there is no way he knew. I mean, he didn't wake up in the operating room and see all this. I mean he was out, and was out for, I don't know, even a day or two while we recovered him in the intensive care unit. So what does that tell you?

Was that his soul up there?" [End Transcript]

— —

Did you notice the last thing Dr. Rudy said? ***"Was that his soul up there?"*** That sends shivers down my spine when I think about what an unbeliever must go through to rationalize what is a matter of fact that cannot be ignored.

Case #3-4: Vicki Umipeg & Brad Barrows
Congenitally Blind from Birth
Both Vicki and Brad were born prematurely and suffered what's known as retrolental fibroplasia (in laymen's terms, they are blind as a bat from birth!)

Anyway, at the age of 22, Vicki was a victim of a terrible car accident where she was ejected from the vehicle (obviously, she wasn't driving; ok, maybe I need a break from all this writing :-P). Her injuries were extensive and life-threatening, and included a skull fracture, concussion, and damage to her neck, back, and one leg. In fact, it took her a full year after being released from the hospital before she could stand upright without the risk of fainting.

Vicki said that she felt herself hover over the operating table where she could vividly see herself laying there. She was particularly happy to see a ring that was on her finger that she had never "*seen*" before. She could describe the surrounding in the room, the colors [which she had never seen color before] of the operating room, shoes of the surgeon and nurses, etc. Vicki could see clearly!

At only 8 years of age, in 1968, Brad came down with a severe case of pneumonia and eventually had severe difficulties breathing. Afterward, he was told by nurses that his heart had stopped, apparently for at least four minutes, and that cardiopulmonary resuscitation (CPR) had been necessary to bring him back.

Like many others, including Vicki, Brad said that he felt himself floating over himself laying in his bed. He said he saw his blind roommate get up from his bed and leave the room to get help (his roommate later confirmed this). Brad then felt himself float up above the roof line of the building he was in. He explained the different colors of the snowbanks that surrounded the building, and even described in detail a street car that went by. Brad could see clearly!

So, how is it that a person who has never "*seen*" anything before accurately explain what things "*looked*" like? Go ahead, I'll wait ☺

But wait, there's more! The study I pulled this information from actually examined 31 qualified respondents to their study!!![xxxiii]

I can't but help of the words to the famous song I so love to sing…
"*Amazing Grace, how sweet the sound, that saved a wretch like me. I was once was lost, but now I'm found. Was BLIND, but now I SEE!*"

Case #4: Viola Horton
During a procedure in a hospital in Augusta, GA, Viola's heart stopped beating. She says she can remember clearly hearing the doctor say, "*I've lost her, she's gone.*" Viola said she had no idea who he was talking about, but then all of the sudden, she felt herself floating above her bed. Soon after, she passed through the sealed door to the operating room where she found her family several floors up from where her body was. She saw her daughter and tried to tell her to go change clothes, but she couldn't get her daughter to notice her. Then she tried to tell her husband the same, but to no avail.

About that time, she noticed her brother-in-law standing there. His next-door neighbor happened to be at the hospital that day, and inquired to her brother-in-law about why he was there. Viola was able to hear the conversation between her brother-in-law and his neighbor; and it went like this:

Neighbor: *What are you doing here today? What are you doing this weekend?*
Brother-in-law: *Well, it looks like my sister-in-law is going to kick the bucket, and I was planning to go to Athens, but I'll stick around now and be a pallbearer.*

Viola was able to ask her brother-in-law about that incident later. She said, "*He didn't want to admit it, but he did admit it is what he had said. And I laughed at him… it embarrassed him.*"[xxxiv]

Moral to the story: If you're going to say something derogatory about someone, you might want to make sure their actually dead! #facepalm

<u>More Than The Eye Can See</u>

Your physical body has a separate entity that cannot be seen; it's called your soul. Your soul does not cease to exist when your physical body stops working. But where it goes is up to you... (I'm getting ahead of myself again).

As the famous philosopher, Pluto, once said,
"We believe, do we not, that death is the separation of the soul from the body, and that the state of being dead is the state in which the body is separated from the soul and exists alone by itself?"[xxxv]

As the Word of God says, *"For this perishable body must put on the imperishable, and this mortal body must put on immortality. When the perishable puts on the imperishable, and the mortal puts on immortality, then shall come to pass the saying that is written:*

"Death is swallowed up in victory."
"O death, where is your victory?
O death, where is your sting?"
The sting of death is sin, and the power of sin is the law. But thanks be to God, who gives us the victory through our Lord Jesus Christ."[xxxvi]

WHY

Are We Here?

> *"First off, I want to start by saying I do not want to downgrade or offend anyone's religious or personal view, so if that happens, then I am sorry. I believe in evolution. We have no meaning to be alive. Humans are not good at all. We have single handedly tore apart this world. If we had meaning, and god truly created us then I believe that he created humans to tear this world apart. There will be no apocalypse for other animals. Everything shall return to the dust from which they came eventually and soon there won't be a single soul to remember what we have done. Therefore, we have no meaning except to live and die."*
>
> - Quote from anonymous atheist on social media

<u>Valedictorian's Speech of 2015</u>

It would be hard for me to read the above statement as a serious position taken by loads of people if it weren't for the time I attended a graduation ceremony at Apalachee High School. I had several students from the youth ministry that I was the pastor over, so I decided to weather the rains and cheer them on as they ventured into the next season of their lives. Now, call me crazy, but I was under the impression that the main purpose of the valedictorian's speech was to come alongside the graduating students as their peer and encourage them to go start adulting. I mean, this is the final sentiment that should inspire and motivate them to go fulfill the purpose for their lives; right?

Well, the speech started out as a tear-jerker. The young lady talked about how important the role her mom played in her life and gave props to all moms out there for giving themselves to the raising of their children. I can only assume that this young lady's dad had not been around, since there was absolutely no mention of him. I found myself with dust flying into my eyes as I recalled how important my own mother used to be in my life. As we all were about to break into a rainy rendition of holding hands and singing Kumbaya, there was a sudden shift felt in the atmosphere as part two of the valedictorian's monumental speech commenced. She started part two by saying, *"As we leave these years of education in our lives, always remember that we will all still be connected no matter where we go..."* Oh boy, here comes the dust in my eyes again. She's about to break into how to maintain friendships and bonds that were developed throughout their school years together. This is going to be some sweet advice that these students really need to listen to. She continued... *"We are all connected, because we are all Star Dust!"* Ahem, what did she just say? *"That's right, evolution is a fact that we have all learned here through our education, and we all know that millions of years ago, our great ancestors were riding on the backs of stars, flying through the universe, until our ancestors rode a crashed star into our now planet Earth, and from all of this, we are here, connected by the fact that we are all descendants of star dust."* I sat there in awe of the total insanity of her statements and annoyed by the irony of a valedictorian's speech including this notion of nonsensical attributions of meaningless.

Again, call me crazy, but how in the world are you supposed to feel like you are about to enter the next phase of your purpose when the valedictorian just told you that you have no absolute meaning because you are really nothing more than a great unguided cosmic accident that randomly occurred millions of years ago? An accident is defined as, *"an unforeseen and unplanned event or circumstance."* If we were to believe that we all came from an unforeseen and unplanned star crash, if our existence weren't purposed and intentional, then where could we derive any purpose for our lives?

The Absurdity of Life Without God

I love board games. Now, don't ask my family about playing them with me because they might make up a lie and tell you that I can be a little, say, aggressive in my competitor's spirit when I'm playing. I'd like to think of my actions as being righteously motivated by the willingness to give everything I've got to play the games with the utmost excellence! Anyway, I think there can be some valuable insights gained when one looks at how games are played. Let's take a look at the game, Monopoly.

Simulated Example:
One day, I extend an invite to you to come over to my house to play a game of Monopoly. You knock on the door; I let you in and tell you to have a seat in the living room. Next, I explain to you that while I go to the kitchen to fix a sandwich for us to eat, you can set the board up ANY way you'd like. As I walk away you think to yourself that you have got this one in the bag. You giggle as you put hotels on Boardwalk and Park Place. You snicker at becoming a Railroad Tycoon. You even LOL because you set up all the money on your side of the board, except for ten $1 bills on my side of the board. You start my piece off in Jail, and you coldly wait for me to come back into the room so you can marvel at my dismay for how perfectly you set the board up to your advantage. I softly enter the room with our two sandwiches in my hands, I place them down on the table, hand you a napkin, and then sit down on my side of the board. You reach for your scrumptious sandwich, lift it towards your mouth to take a bite, when all of the sudden I kick my foot into the bottom of the game board, sending the contents of the board flying though the room! You look at me with a strange confusion washed over your face as I lean back in my chair and start to eat. I sit up quickly and instruct you to go ahead and set the board up again as I go to fix us something to drink to go with our sandwiches. Begrudgingly, you collect all the contents of the game and methodically set the board back up the way you had it set up the first time. As I walk back into the room, I hand you your drink, and then

proceed to use my arm to wipe the entire game off the table. At this, you stand up and yell, *"Hey, what's your problem?"* I politely ask what you mean by that. You then attempt to explain to me that I am in the wrong for demolishing the hard work you have put into the game. In response, I look at you with a confused look and ask how my actions were wrong. You see, up until this point, I have been playing the game without instructions and you were only following my instructions. I was simply allowing you to make up the rules for set up, and then I was making up the rule that I could beat you by destroying your work. At this, you do an epic face-palm, and tell me that there are rules that we should both be following. *"Rules; what Rules?"* I exclaim. You then go to the game box, pull out the rules book, and throw them at me as I proclaim, *"Oh, I see now. There is actually a point to this game?"*

Here's the thing. Before any rules or a point to the game was established, you and I were engaged in one meaningless event after another. It was meaningless for you to set the board up any way you wanted. It was meaningless for me to kick the game over. It was meaningless for you to reset the board, and it was meaningless for me to wipe it out with my arm. We were both trapped in one meaningless event after another meaningless event (have I mentioned the word, meaningless?) It was absurd for either of us to try and have a meaningful game together. It wasn't until you introduced a set of rules that led to the game having a meaning, or a means to an end that we both started to assign value to the way we would now play the game. Since you didn't create the game, you can't make up the rules. When you create your own game, then, and only then can you dictate the rules that must be followed. Parker Brothers created Monopoly in 1935, and only Parker Brothers has the right to assign the rules. So it goes with the universe, and all that is in it. When you create a universe, you get to make the rules. So far, we have learned that it is God who intelligently created the universe, and all that is in it. And since He created it, He gets the right to make the rules.

Without God, life is meaningless because a purely physical, accidental, blind, and unguided existence emits no point to anything at all. However, as soon as we understand that there is a rule Maker, we begin to see that there is an absolute meaning behind the fabric of our lives. Our understanding of the game of real life starts to take shape as we study the book of instructions written by our Maker about how we are to live and breathe and spend our time while visiting here on planet earth.

> **Note:** February 19, 2018
> I just got finished watching one of the primary hearings for Nikolas Cruz, the gunman who murdered 17 people at the Parkland, FL school shooting last week (as of this writing). Social media has been in uproar with democrats blaming the NRA, republicans blaming the democrats, the race card has been played, social activists who support abortion have been in a full court press to ban guns in order to save children [oh, the irony there]. Students are threatening to walk out of school, conveniently on April 20th (national pot smoking day) unless law makers come up with a solution for gun control. All of these things make people feel like they are serving their civil duties as they pompously place a hero's award on their social justice's mantle as though they really accomplished anything at all. And by next week, they will be on to another social injustice looking for yet another internet warrior participation trophy for their mantle.
>
> Let's again apply deductive reasoning to everyone's above arguments
> **A)** No inanimate object has the power to move to cause harm on its own without intervention.
> **B)** All guns, trucks, planes, and rocks are inanimate objects.

C) Therefore, guns, trucks, planes, and rocks have no power to cause harm on their own without intervention.

The GUN that Nikolas used to murder 17 people was NOT the problem! The TRUCK used to plow into a crowd, murdering 10 people in New York City was NOT the problem! The PLANES used to murder 2,997 on September 11th was NOT the problem! The ROCK that Cain used to murder Able as recorded in the book of Genesis was NOT the problem! The lack of God's direction is the problem. Let me explain.

Evil and Free Will

We already covered why God created us with freewill in the first A.D.D. sidenote on page 53, but I want to take a brief moment to unpack a different perspective on the meaning of Free Will.

I was standing in line at McDonalds one day as I glanced around the room to see a young woman wearing a shirt that read:

Dear God,
Why do you allow violence in schools?
Signed, Concerned Student

Dear Concerned Student,
I'm not allowed in schools.
Signed, God

I remember thinking to myself how profound that thought was, so I began to seek out just how logical the application of this truth could be. What I found was nothing short of a game-changer in the way that I looked at things that were surrounding me, but also inwardly as I examined my own life in regards to the areas that I have given God full access to vs. those areas that I'm still holding onto.

It was while I was watching an incredible teaching on *"The Power of Music"* that my friend, Montell Jordan, was teaching on that I truly understood the true nature of evil. Montell was using a pen to illustrate a powerful truth about good vs. evil. He picked up a pen held it in the air and asked the question, *"Does this pen have any power in and of itself? Of course not."* He went on to explain that the person in control of the pen has the power to either write encouraging words that will bless someone else (a.k.a: Good), or they can choose to use that same pen to write a nasty letter full of bitterness and hate to another person (a.k.a: Evil). It is strictly up to the person holding the pen as to whether or not they will use their own free will to either bless or curse with that pen. The pen is powerless.

There is no such a thing as cold!

You can have lots of heat, even more heat, super-heat, mega-heat, white heat, a little heat, or no heat. But we don't have anything called *"cold."* We can hit 458 degrees below zero, which is no heat, but we can't go any further after that. There is no such thing as cold, otherwise we would be able to go colder than 458. Cold is only a word we use to describe the absence of heat. We cannot measure cold. Heat we can measure in thermal units because heat is energy. Cold is not the opposite of heat, just the absence of it.

There is there no such a thing as darkness! Darkness is not something, it is the absence of something. You can have low light, normal light, bright light, flashing light, etc. But if you have no light constantly you have nothing, and it's called darkness. That's the word we made up to define the absence of light. Death is not the opposite of life, merely the absence of it. Evil is not the opposite of good, merely the absence of it.

We are designed to give love and be loved. We are designed to have intimate relationships with other people, and that's what God desires from us. His greatest desire is for us to *"love Him with all our heart and with all our soul and with all our mind and with all our strength."*xxxvii We are not designed for pre-packaged church services, or prayer chants. God wants our hearts to turn toward Him, and to love Him enough to care about what His thoughts are toward us. When we realize that *"His thoughts are not our thoughts, neither are our ways His ways. For as the heavens are higher than the earth, so His ways are higher than our ways and His thoughts than our thoughts..."*xxxviii

You see, I have some great news for you – you never have to be God! You never have to feel like the weight of the world is on you alone because God tells us to, *"Be strong and courageous. Do not fear or be in dread of them, for it is the LORD your God who goes with you. He will not leave you or forsake you."*xxxix Jesus literally says, *"Come to me, all who are weary and burdened, and I will give you rest. Take my yoke upon you, and learn from me, for I am gentle and lowly in heart, and you will find rest for your souls. For my yoke is easy, and my burden is light."*xl Look, I'm not telling you that life isn't going to throw you curve balls, but you don't have to strike out at the plate either. It is absolutely possible to let Jesus be your batting coach.

Wrap Your Mind Around This [if you can]

Genesis 1:1

"In the beginning, God created the heavens and the earth." We have already learned that time had a definite beginning from the Kalam Cosmological Argument. Genesis 1:1 isn't saying that when God created all that we see, He was creating the first moment *"in"* time; it is saying that He created the first moment *"of"* time. Before Genesis 1:1, time did not exist. As fun as that is to think about, it only gets more exciting when we read two of my very favorite verses in all of scripture:

Ephesians 1:4
"Even as He chose us in Him BEFORE the foundation of the world, that we should be holy and blameless before Him."

Ephesians 2:10
"For we are God's workmanship, created in Christ Jesus for good works, which God prepared in BEFOREHAND, that we should walk in them."

The bible makes it clear that *"in Him [Jesus] all things were created, things in heaven and on earth, visible and invisible, whether thrones or dominions or rulers or authorities. All things were created through Him and for Him. He is before all things, and in Him all things hold together."*[xli] So when we read in Ephesians, *"He chose in in Him"* – *"created in Christ Jesus…"* what we are seeing is that we are literally a creation of Christ Jesus. Let me make an illustration for you.

What Creates Value in Something?

If I were to offer you a twenty-dollar bill, you would take it (not that you're a free-loader or something. I mean, who wouldn't want a free Jackson?). You instinctively trust that you could go to the store and buy some delicious ice cream with that twenty because it has value to it. What if I were to take that same twenty and tear a small rip in it – maybe burn a tiny hole in it – throw it on the ground and step on it; get it dirty – even rub it under my armpits or something. That same twenty is now dirty, stinky, torn, burned, etc. Would you still take it? Of course, you would. I mean you were already fantasizing about that yummy ice cream! You see, it doesn't matter how badly the twenty had been damaged, its value never changed because its value is not in the paper it's printed on. The twenty is valuable because of what is behind its creation! The gold standard that backs that piece of paper is what gives it its value.

It's the same for you and me. Our value is not defined by how many times we've been burned in life, or how many times our hearts have been torn, or how dirty our poor choices (sins) have made us, or that we stink with the smell of a fallen and depraved world. No, our value comes from something that is beyond us. Our value comes from Who created us. You're value can't be bought or sold by anyone or anything because it is totally defined by the One who already *"bought you for a price."*[xlii] Oh how sweet it is to know that we are bought and protected by the One who defines the very essence of love, grace, mercy, and forgiveness; that is *IF* we let Him.

<u>Before What?</u>

Notice that the two verses in Ephesians both mentions *"before"* and *"beforehand."* Verse 1: 4 makes it absolutely clear that before God even spoke the universe into existence, creating the first moment of time, before time began, Christ Jesus prepared good works that we should walk in them blamelessly and in holiness. BEFORE! If that doesn't make your head explode, you didn't read what it said. Let me give you the DGV (Dave Glander Version) of these two texts combined into one glorious truth:

"Before time existed and the creation of everything we see, God knew exactly when you would come along in your mother's womb to make your grand entrance onto the stage of life. Because He created you in His [Jesus Christ] image, you have a value and a purpose in your life that cannot be taken away from you. That purpose is to walk out a good life, full of good works that you can accomplish, should you choose to accept this mission. Before God created anything, He had already created a life for you!"[xliii]

BOOM! That just happened! I didn't make up one word of that up that can't be found in scripture which is true about you, even the *"before I formed you in the womb, I knew you."*[xliv]

A.D.D. break for a reading portion of an awesome and relevant Psalm:

"For you formed my inward parts; you knitted me together in my mother's womb. I praise you, for I am fearfully and wonderfully made. Wonderful are your works; my soul knows it very well. My frame was not hidden from you, when I was being made in secret, intricately woven in the depths of the earth. Your eyes saw my unformed substance; in your book were written, every one of them, <u>the days that were formed for me</u>, when as yet there was none of them. How precious to me are your thoughts, O God! How vast is the sum of them!"[xlv]

"...the days that were formed for me..." Let that sink in for a moment.

Did you do it? Did you take a moment to let that sink in? Well, what are you waiting for? *"He says, 'Be still, and know that I am God.'"*[xlvi]

Ok, now that we've taken a minute to let that sink in, lets unpack that one a bit. You matter so much to God that He literally spent energy thinking about you so much that He formed days just for YOU! Think about it like this; what if I told you that I was going to take you to Hawaii for a couple of weeks for a vacation, but you have two options. Option A would be that we would have limited funds to get around, and we would have no time to research what to do, volcanoes to see, where to eat, where the best (local) beaches would be, and we wouldn't have access to google to figure it out once we got there – we would just have to wing it. Now, I'm an adventurous, spontaneous person, so I think I could make the best of it and still have a good time. However, there's another option.

Option B would be that we would be able to go with my best friend who lives there, who knows all the best food stops, beaches, volcanoes, tropical rain forests. Because we would be with him, our limited budget wouldn't matter because we would stay in his mansion, and he would bring us in his vehicle to all the places that we would go to. We would be so full from our experience that we would literally be ready for it to end so we can go share our experiences with others.

Which option would you choose? I know at least one of you is *"that guy"* or *"gal"* who is a smart butt who just thought you would be so cool as to think to yourself; Option A. Well, you may be an idiot! As for the rest of us wise folks, Option B is the obvious choice. Option B was already predetermined to be a raving success because it had a Planner already hand-picked for the journey that would guarantee we would see and do way more than we could've ever imagined!

Soooooo... I think you know where I'm going with all of this. Option A represents our choice to try and live this journey out on our own. We have limited resources and no google. Option B represents us making a conscious decision (a.k.a.: Free Will) to follow Christ's leadership as the One who preplanned and formed days just for you. Is it really something we need to ponder, or is it as obvious as it seems? It saddens me when I see so many people try and tell God that they have a better plan. Every time I see this I watch through time as that person's life is like a hamster wheel. They keep running, and running, and running, and running, yet they never seem to get anywhere.

Here's the hard truth – in both verses of Ephesians, it says that we *"should"* walk in them, not that we will. Whether we choose (a.k.a.: Free Will) to walk in the plans that God purposes us to walk in is fully up to us. Just because someone may choose (a.k.a.: Free Will) to not walk in obedience to their Creator doesn't make what their Creator said to be false. What God told us He did for us stands for us to choose (a.k.a.: Free Will) as we may. God is a gentleman, He never forces Himself on anyone, rather He *"stands at the door [of our hearts and minds] and knocks. If anyone hears His voice and opens the door, He will come in and eat with that person, and they with Him.*"xlvii

Notice it doesn't say that He kicks open the door like a police raid. Sadly, some will be too asleep to hear His voice, or will be too proud to open the door and they will miss the grand tour of Hawaii (a.k.a.: Life now and eternal)

Let Me Brag On God

What I'm about to share with you is not out of any pride or arrogance. To prove that I have to remind you of how lost, hopeless, shattered, addicted, perverted, frustrated, angry, bitter, and lost I was at the beginning of this story, as told in my opening chapter. All of those definitions of who my identity was before I met Jesus accomplished nothing but loss, heartache, betrayal, hurt, distrusts, financial ruin, and almost took my very life. So, everything from here on out is what GOD has done in and through my life, and not a single ounce of credit can go to me. The ONLY thing I've done, and am still doing to this day, is using my FREE WILL to choose to trust that His leadership is better than mine, every time and in every way. As I said earlier, it is an awesome peace to know that I never have to be god again, as I was doing before I met Him that nearly killed me.

Since the day I was saved from myself, through His grace and mercy, I have done things that I never could've imagined possible. One of my biggest dreams when I was a child was to fly a plane. Well, not only did God allow me to do this several times now, but He blew my mind when he brought me to speak at an Apologetics Conference in Nags Head, North Carolina – the very place where flight was birthed. I got the chance to fly up there with my wife and dear friends, Ken and Helen, in Ken's private plane. We landed at First Flight Airport and the plane stopped approximately 30 yards from the stone that commemorates the very first successful flight conducted by the Wright Brothers in 1903! Talk about taking my breath away and God ***"giving me the desires of my heart."***[xlviii] I was literally happier than a fat kid in a candy store!

One time I ended up at an elite conference in Atlanta, helping a legend in the world of apologetics, Gary Habermas. Because I was there I ran into a gentleman that was a higher-up at a huge Christian ministry in the Cincinnati area. He must have mistaken me for someone of much greater importance (meaning they are looking for presidents of universities and highly influential Christian leaders of major ministries around the world) because he invited me to go on a Christian Leaders Trip through the Grand Canyon. When I got the invite and was requested to put down an earnest deposit of only $300 (the balance of $4,700 was paid through a sponsorship!), I called my good friend, Dr. Bird, and asked him what he knew about this opportunity. This is how the conversation went:

Dr. Bird: *"You mean you got an invite for that trip?!"*

Me: *"Yes."*

Dr. Bird: *"GO pay the deposit and secure your spot before they figure out who you are!!!"*

Bwahahahaha!!! Dr. Bird wasn't being mean, and I did exactly what he said to do. The reality is that I should've never been on that trip with the qualifications I had at the time. But God! He wanted me on that trip to expose me to some folks that have been absolutely essential to my ministry. When I tell you that going through the Grand Canyon from start to nearly finish on a raft full of scholars being led by one of the best geologists in the world, over 8 days and 197 river miles, through 6 Class TEN rapids... words escape me. But God!

I have been blessed enough to have traveled to many states to speak and teach at conferences, schools, universities, churches, retreats, and camps. I have shared the same platform with people who have more letters after their name than the alphabet, some of whom hold multiple PhD's! Remember what I said about my educational achievements back in my testimony? Yeah, But GOD! If you ever think you're not good enough to be of any use, look at me. I am NO different, better, or loved by God than you are. The only difference between you and me may be that I have unlocked the truth of what it's like to be sold out and trust that God is better at being God than I am.

I have hosted my own apologetics radio show. I have been the guest on multiple TV talk shows, radio shows, and podcasts. I am a published contributor to one of the largest homeschool magazines in the country. I have published an apologetics curriculum called, "Faith Survival Guide." I am the founder of one of the premier apologetics camps in the country called, Equip Retreat. I have been a youth pastor and now have started a church that I co-pastored for many years. I travel in an RV around the country with my dear friend, Scott Knies, as we minister together all over the place. My ministry journeys have taken me to the ocean several times. I've met some of the greatest people in God's kingdom. I have built an 1,800 square foot museum that holds over 300 ancient artifacts, over 50 ancient Bible leaves with some of the rarest on display. There's 3900-year-old cuneiform, a massive modern Israel history collection, and I was able to purchase at next to nothing, 1 of only 5 digital S.T.U.R.P. Team recreations of the Shroud of Turin in the world.

God has used my testimony to free other kids that were in the bondage of sexual molestation, and adults who never dealt with what happened to them. I have seen addicts set free. I have prayed with many to receive eternal life through the Gospel of Jesus Christ. I have had the opportunity to marry some and preach the burial of others. I have been a part of seeing lives and relationships restored through God.

God has restored my passion and ability for music, and I have been leading worship for the last 7 years, not only at my church, but other places of worship, conferences, retreats, etc. When I was in the world living for myself, the main thing I wanted to do was play music – well, guess what? But God!

Oh yeah, the best part is that God completely restored me to my family. My wife and I are not just married still, but best friends and ministry partners. My son is awesome and has his dream job already at the age of only 21. He plays drums on the worship team with me (there's nothing like worshiping God with your family!). Oh, that brings on another point; he gave me the daughter I always wanted by marrying Alyssa, who is one of the most incredible worship leaders that I know of (and that's not being biased!). And I also get to lead worship with her, and my wife runs the lyrics for the congregation; so it's a total family endeavor!!!

Are you picking up what I'm putting down? Do you smell what I'm stepping in? Look at what has happened to my life after I found the true meaning of life. And you know what… God is waiting for you to make the same choice. He doesn't call the equipped. He equips the called!

I literally changed nothing in my old, wretched life other than worshipping, trusting, and following in obedience the will that God has for my life. It really is that simple; don't over-complicate it! I can guarantee that when you choose to fully surrender your will to His, you will see over time that it is the best decision you have ever made. Things won't change overnight. It took you some time to get where you are currently at, and it's going to take Him some time to undo some of the things you have chosen to do. Give it time. Life is not a sprint, it's an endurance race.

"Do you not know that in a race all the runners run, but only one gets the prize? Run in such a way as to get the prize."[xlix]
– The Apostle Paul

If I hold out that twenty-dollar bill, and you never take it from my hand, you will never own the value of what it can do for you. If you never open yourself fully to His will, you will never accomplish the full purpose of your formed days that you could have.

You can take this next promise to the bank:

"For I know the plans I have for you, declares the LORD, plans to prosper you and not to harm you, plans to give you a hope and a future."[1] – God

Conclusion: noun
con·clu·sion|\kən-'klü-zhən
A Reasoned Judgment

What does this ultimately mean?

I never get surprised by the timing in which God brings things to pass in our lives. Afterall, He created the stars, the moon, and the sun to dance to a perfect beat through our skies in such a way that we can actually study them to know the seasons.[li] Since His mighty power is enough to guide thousands of years of planetary motion in complete perfection, it's quite a simple thing for God to arrange perfect timing in our lives when we are fully submitted to His perfect will.

As I write, I am sitting in the hospital room with my brother as we do our best to comfort my dad as he is passing from this life to the next. There is nothing coincidental about my writing this chapter on concluding the end of this book as we are currently sitting here faced with the inevitability of our own mortality as the air of death permeates the room. As Benjamin Franklin put so clearly – *"In this world, nothing is certain except death and taxes."*[lii] One day, each of us will breathe our last breath of borrowed air. What happens next is up to you.

One Minute After You Die

"It is destined for man to die once, and after that comes judgment."[liii] Did you notice something key about what the Bible just had to say? It literally says, *"destined... to die **once**..."* [emphasis mine]. Take note with the use of the word *"once."*
When we leave this place we call earth, we will have one of two destinations that we will all go to. For some, the minute after we die will be the most glorious thing we have ever seen. I mean, things

that cannot be fathomed with our current eyes and minds will one day be experienced by those who chose to be there. For others, the experience won't be nearly as pleasant. Let's go ahead and spend a brief moment on the other location that one may choose to go to upon their death.

<u>What In The Hell Is Going On?</u>

Hell wasn't created for a single human being to ever enter. The Bible makes it clear that hell was created as *"the eternal fire prepared for the devil and his angels."*[liv] The idea that any one person is desired to go to this awful place is contrary to the Word of God. God literally says that He *"does not wish that any [humans] should perish, but that all should reach repentance [be saved]."*[lv]

There are two things that you need to understand:
1) Hell is real.
2) God has no desire for you to go there!

Remember when we talked about you being a "triune" being? That you were specially created, set apart from the rest of creation. That you have a body, soul, and spirit. Well, your body will one day die, but your soul will continue for all of eternity. Without the completion of having the third part of you, the Spirit within you, your soul will go to spend eternity in Hell. Hell is literally a place where God does not and cannot exist. After one is sent to Hell, there is no chance for repentance, and therefore no chance at being with God for eternity. I don't know exactly what Hell will be like and I'm not going to try. All I know is that, for me, to think of that a third part of me never being complete and there never being a chance for that to be completed IS Hell! We were created to love and have a relationship with our Creator. To think that there will be a place where that is no longer an option IS Hell. Some have attempted to describe what Hell may be like, but all I know is that the thought of being apart from my Creator, Savior, Redeemer, and friend for all eternity, with no chance for parole IS HELL!

The Bible refers to Hell as a dark place where there will be weeping and gnashing of teeth. A place of torment and emptiness.

Why Would A Good God Send Someone To Place Like Hell?

See, here's the thing. I get that argument a lot. People will try to throw that at me like some sort of a checkmate maneuver or something, like they have this irrefutable charge against God and therefore are justified in their denial of Him. But here's the problem with that argument; God doesn't send anyone to Hell, they choose to send themselves. There will be those, and unfortunately, a lot of those, who have made up their mind that they KNOWINGLY choose to reject Jesus Christ while they are alive on planet earth. Therefore, how extremely terrible would it be for God to force someone to spend eternity with Him when they spent a lifetime of not wanting anything to do with Him? That would make Him an unjust God who doesn't care about the free will of those who have chosen that they do not want Him.

We are all going to die a physical death one day. And we shouldn't be fearful of that death because *"We are confident, then, and would prefer to be away from the body and at home with the Lord."*[lvi] The first death is one that will bring us from this existence to the next. What we must make sure of is that while we are here on earth in this *"trial run"* setting, that we are to make the most of our time and that we have made things right with our Creator through the redemptive work that His Son, Jesus, who made it possible for us to be reconciled to our God.

It is the second death that we should fear. *"He who has an ear, let him hear what the Spirit says to the churches. The one who is victorious will not be harmed by the second death."*[lvii]

The Gospel of Jesus Christ

The word gospel is derived from the Anglo-Saxon term god-spell, meaning *"good story,"* a rendering of the Latin evangelium and the Greek euangelion, meaning *"good news"* or *"good telling."* The Gospel literally means GOOD NEWS!!!

I've taken a little break from writing since my dad passed in October. Boy, has it been a roller coaster of events that immediately began to unravel as soon as I got back home from tending to my dad's passing. Nonetheless, I inherited his little Jack Russell, Jackie. She was supposed to be 14 years old according to my brother, but her paperwork that surfaced [after I committed] showed her to only be 8 years old. Whoopie! Got me on that one, dad... hehehe. She's sweet; hyper, but sweet, and my wife finally has a tiny little lap dog so happy wife, happy life, right?

Anyway, since October, there's been a lot that has happened. Probably the most memorable of all will be COVID-19. COVID shut the entire world down. People were forced to stay home. Mom and Pops businesses closed because they couldn't afford to stay open without patrons. Restaurants had to deliver because they couldn't have people in their places of business. Parents became teachers in an instant because kids couldn't go to school. I could go on and on, but what stood out most is how sad everyone was [is] (I'm finishing this book in September 2020). Everywhere you look, people are covered with face masks and their eyes look sad. This, on top of rioting and cities burning all over the United States. It's CRAZY out there. I never would have thought in my 46 years on earth, that I would see what's happening all around us.

In the midst of everything going on, even in your own life right now... right where you're sitting, wouldn't it be nice to just receive some good news? How about some great news? That's what I thought! Well, let me tell you something great!

The Garden of Eden

Whenever someone asks me if I really believe in a literal Adam and Eve, I without hesitation say, *"Of Course!"* When I read the accounts in Genesis of the fall of mankind and then I look around at the world we live in, I can't help but think of how simply, yet eloquently, the Bible narrates the overarching problem of mankind. It takes the brilliance of God to be able to nail down ALL of man's problems in one short narrative! If a man were to have made up a story, he would've made it far too wordy and complex, and then still would've missed the target. Also, study out *"Mitochondrial Eve"* to see the scientific explanation of all of us coming from one single woman. I'll attach a link here for you to study: [https://genesisapologetics.com/faqs/genesis-and-genetics-dna-clocks-exactly-confirm-recent-creation/]

The reason why the biblical account of Adam and Eve is so important is because that is the first place God addressed the Good News that was to come for ALL of us! The original sin that was committed that caused all of humanity to be separated from the perfect relationship that we should have had with our Creator was not when Adam ate from the forbidden tree. No, it was when Adam allowed the questioning of God's character into his mind. God said to Adam, *"you must not eat from the tree of the knowledge of good and evil, for when you eat from it you will certainly die."*[xlviii] That was pretty plain and simple, and yes, the day that Adam ate from the tree, he died; not physically, but Spiritually. Adam went from being a perfect creation of God, having a body, soul, and spirit, to only being a body with a soul. The spirit inside of Adam died, and that death of the spirit has been passed down to every one of the descendants of Adam. We are all born *"still-born,"* spiritually speaking.

A.D.D. Rabbit Trail Moment

When I held to my atheistic worldview, I had one major flaw in my theory. I would watch those who had all I ever wanted. People like Jerry Garcia, Kurt Cobain, Shannon Hoon, etc. all had the fame, fortunes, instruments, girls, drugs, travel, etc. They had everything I could ever want. But then I kept watching Jerry go in and out of rehabs until he finally died of just too much drug abuse on his body. Kurt shot himself, and Shannon overdosed. Add them to the list of others before them, Jimmy Hendrix, Janis Joplin, Jim Morrison, Marilyn Monroe, John Belushi, and the list went on. I couldn't figure out why they were overdosing and/or committing suicide if they had it all! I always thought, let me have what they had, and I'll prove that it can satisfy the soul!

Well, it wasn't until I met Jesus and received His Holy Spirit, that it finally dawned on me. What each one of those individuals were trying to do, was the same thing that nearly killed me. We were all trying to fill that void that Adam left us with other things. Unfortunately for them, they never found the ONLY thing that can truly fill that void and make one fully complete as they were originally intended and designed to live as. The only thing that can fill that void is being filled [and completed] with the Holy Spirit of God. The Bible tells us that when we accept and receive Jesus as our personal Savior, that God *"sets His seal of ownership on us, and puts His Spirit in our hearts as a deposit, guaranteeing what is to come."*[lix] When you are saved, God literally places His Spirit inside of you filling that hole that causes so much grief and emptiness. No longer will that empty hole cause strife within you, for you will finally be complete in form, as you have always meant to be! Isn't that great news!!!

Back To Our Originally Scheduled Broadcast

> *Wait, do you have a hole you've been trying to fill? School, Career, Relationship, Kids, Money, Drugs, Porn, Alcohol?*

Ok, Now Back To Our Originally Scheduled Broadcast

Again, it wasn't Adam eating the fruit, it was when Adam listened to a deceptive twist from the father of lies.[lx] Pay careful attention here because this is how the devil works. *"He said to the woman, "Did God **really** say, 'You must not eat from any tree in the garden'?"*[lxi] Did you catch it? Satan asked Eve, *"Did God **really** say..."* That was the seed of doubt in God's character that led to Adam eating of the fruit also. Was God really going to do what He said He would do? Was what He said really going to happen, or was God just making an empty threat? Satan sowed a seed, and then once Adam [and Eve] bought into the seeds of his deception, he [Satan] dropped the finality of his lie. He said, *"'You will not certainly die,' the serpent said to the woman."*[lxii]

The account goes on to say that Adam and Eve noticed their nakedness and were ashamed of what they had done. They had sinned against the Creator. They attempted to fix the problem of their sin by covering their nakedness; *"so they sewed fig leaves together and made coverings for themselves,"*[lxiii] but their attempts were futile. Now watch this: After their feeble attempt to fix their problem themselves, God stepped in to fix it for them. *"The Lord God made garments of skin for Adam and his wife and clothed them.*"[lxiv] It was **only** by the shedding of innocent blood that the animal's skin could be used to clothe or cover their nakedness. And did you notice that the first attempt, they did for ***"themselves,"*** whereas the shed blood was *for* ***"them."*** Adam did not shed that innocent blood; God did!

Back To The Future - Again

Wrap your mind around this for a moment. The reason why Jesus HAD TO be born of a Virgin was because the curse was passed down through Adam's seed, not Eve's. God held Adam in contempt on that sad day; not Eve.[lxv] When Mary conceived Jesus, it was not through the seed of man, so the sin curse was not passed onto him.[lxvi] Had Jesus been born of Joseph's seed [His earthly *"father"*], He would not have been able to lead the sinless life that He did.

God knew all along that Adam was going to sin and that He would have to come to the rescue of man in order to fix the problem.[lxvii] We also see this model when Abraham went to take Isaac to be sacrificed. To test Abraham's obedience, God asked Abraham to sacrifice his only son, Isaac, but watch what happens. When Isaac asked where the lamb for the sacrifice was, Abraham replied, *"My son, God will provide himself a lamb for a burnt offering."*[lxviii] Did you catch that? God HIMSELF will be the lamb. Jesus is referred to in many cases as the Lamb that was slain![lxix] 2,500 years before Jesus was even born, God was painting the picture of what His eventual arrival and mission would look like so that those paying attention would know it was Him (by the way, the Bible is FULL of incredible tidbits like this). The theme of God being the One to fix our sin nature was, and always has been the plan. That is one of the defining points about the difference between Christianity and EVERY other worldview. Every other worldview is based on the merits of the person's own ability to perform said duties in order to be counted worthy. Christianity is the ONLY worldview that claims that we cannot do this for ourselves. Only God can save us and make us worthy (remember the $20 bill?).

Jesus lived a perfect life in His approximate 30 plus year span here. He was tempted, tried, and persecuted. He was arrested, beaten, spit on, and nailed to a cross where He died a horrible gruesome death. But why? Why did God choose this method? It's simple, really. Our sin problem that separates us from God isn't a small problem; it's a huge problem. Huge problems need huge solutions. Someone has to pay God for all of the sins committed against Him, or else all of eternity would be just as bad as it is here on earth where people are killing each other, robbing each other, slandering each other, and moreover making a mockery of God's holy creation.

If someone were to steal your car, wouldn't you want to see them have to pay for their crime, or would you just sit back and say, nah, that's alright. What about if someone murdered your loved one; should they go to jail, or just be allowed to walk free to do it again? See, we all naturally understand that when a law is broken, punishment, to some degree, is necessary for proper justification. And we also understand that there are degrees of punishment based upon the level of the crim committed. So, when we think about our lives, we understand that some sort of punishment, or payment, must be made to the Creator for violating His rules (remember, you didn't create the Monopoly game or the universe).

Let's say you got busted doing 60mph in a school zone. You go to court and the district attorney lets you know that your fine will be somewhere around $5,000. Your sitting there wondering where in the world you're going to come up with that kind of cash. You are right about to walk up and face the judge, when all of the sudden this man gets up, walks over, and whispers something to the judge. The judge looks at you and says, *"This man is offering to pay your fine in total and wipe your record clean."* What would you do? Of course, you would take the offer. Naturally, you would want to know why the man was offering it to you, but you'd be a fool to not accept the offer. The man reaches out to you with fifty hundred-dollar bills… what do you have to do? Ah, you are so stinking smart! You HAVE TO ACT!!! You have to reach out and TAKE the offer in order to take possession of the offer and use it to pay your fine. If you just stand there and do nothing, you won't be the recipient of the offer, and then you'd still be facing payment on your own.

I have some bad news, and some GREAT news for you. The fine you owe the Creator is too much for you to ever pay. The only way for you to pay for it is if you never sinned [broken one of His rules] a single time in your whole life.

3 Questions

1) Have you ever told a lie? Even a small one.
   What does that make you? A ___Liar___.
2) Have you ever taken something that didn't belong to you? Even like a pencil off a desk that wasn't yours.
   What does that make you? A ___Theif___.
3) Have you ever looked at another with lustful thoughts? Jesus said you committed adultery the second you did.
   What does that make you? An ___Adulterer___.

So, by your own admission (I didn't call you that, you said this about yourself), you are a lying, adulterous thief! When you face the JUDGE (God), and He asks if you are worthy to enter based on your sinless life, do you think He's going to let you in based on your above admissions? Again, we all understand the concept of paying a penalty for breaking a law. Without going any further, you admitted to breaking AT LEAST 3 of God's most basic laws.

But here's the Great News! Jesus paid ALL of your fines for you. He willfully laid down His perfectly lived life on the cross so that you could be made in right standing with your Creator. He paid it ALL! But what do you have to do? You HAVE TO ACT! You have to accept that you have sinned against the laws of God, and that you would like to put your trust in Jesus Christ to pay God for your fines that you rightfully owe Him for breaking His laws.

It's really that simple. Don't overcomplicate things! Becoming a Christian is simply trusting in Jesus Christ for your salvation. And when you do, the Holy Spirit moves back inside you which makes you complete once and for all. Everything that you've ever needed will now be accomplished and a sense of peace will follow you. It doesn't mean every world problem will now be solved. It took you some years to get where you are, but with God, He can take you places you've never dreamed possible. I am a living, walking, talking, breathing example of that.

You want to do it? You want to trust Jesus with your everlasting soul and be born again; born of the Spirit, and not just body and soul? There's nothing magical to say, but I'll help you out. Say this and mean it; trust it.

"God. I realize I have sinned against You. I'm sorry. I ask for Your forgiveness right now. I am placing my trust in what Your Son, Jesus Christ, accomplished for me on that cross. I take hold of the salvation that He is offering. I take hold of the payment that only Jesus could make for me. I thank you for giving me Your Holy Spirit to guide me from this day forth. I am now a child of the Living God and understand my true value now. In Jesus' name I pray. Amen."

If you prayed that prayer just now, please let me know by sending me an email at Dave@TruthMinistries.tv. I would like to make sure you get plugged into your new life in Christ. It's literally the best decision you've EVER made!!!

Find you a good church that you're comfortable in. Read the bible. It's not a competition. Read it slowly and digest it. I'd suggest starting with the Gospel of John. It's the fourth book in the New Testament. Make prayer a regular thing. There's no fancy way to talk to God, just talk to Him like He's your friend, because He is. Hang around good influence with like-minded people who are trying to be more like Christ. Trust me, that's a good move. As my former pastor always said, *"It's the outside voices that helps you make the choices."* Your circle will have a lot to do with your walk in life.

And oh yea, about that why would someone offer to pay your fine thing… It's because He loves you more than you know. And I love you. I told you at the beginning of this journey to discover truth that I loved you, and now I hope you see that too. When you discover just how much God loves you and is for you, it's easy to love a stranger, too. But heck, I've never met a stranger, just someone I haven't hugged yet.

"The Lord bless you
and keep you;
the Lord make His face shine upon you
and be gracious unto you;
the Lord turn His face toward you
and give you peace."[lxx]

Love,
Dave Glander

[i] Ibn Ishaq p. 106

[ii] Sahih Hadith of Bukhari [2] – volume 9, number 111

[iii] Quran 17:47, Quran 25:8

[iv] Life Itself, New York: Simon & Schuster, 1981, P. 88

[v] https://www.merriam-webster.com/dictionary/abiogenesis

[vi] Flowers, C., A Science Odyssey: 100 Years of Discovery, William Morrow and Company, New York, p. 173, 1998

[vii] http://webstersdictionary1828.com/Dictionary/science

[viii] https://en.oxforddictionaries.com/definition/metaphysics

[ix] https://www.merriam-webster.com/dictionary/science

[x] Baruch A. Shalev, *100 Years of Nobel Prizes* (2003), Atlantic Publishers &Distributors , p.57: between 1901 and 2000 reveals that 654 Laureates belong to 28 different religion Most (65.4%) have identified Christianity in its various forms as their religious preference.

[xi] New York NY: Simon & Schuster, 1981, p. 88

[xii] https://www.dailymail.co.uk/sciencetech/article-1294341/Chicken-really-DID-come-egg-say-scientists.html

[xiii] 348 Charles Darwin, The Origin of Species: A Facsimile of the First Edition, Harvard University Press, 1964, p. 189.

[xiv] Isaiah 62:3

[xv] Genesis 1:27

[xvi] 1 Corinthians 2:2

[xvii] 1 Corinthians 9:22

[xviii] Acts 17:17

[xix] Romans 1:19-20

[xx] Genesis 1:27

[xxi] https://www.princeton.edu/~achaney/tmve/wiki100k/docs/Physicalism.html

[xxii] J.B.S. Haldane, Possible Worlds

[xxiii] Mystery of the Mind: A Critical Study of Consciousness (1975)

[xxiv] Luke 10:27

[xxv] Romans 12:2

[xxvi] Romans 8:6

[xxvii] Colossians 3:2

[xxviii] https://www.heart.org/en/health-topics/heart-attack/diagnosing-a-heart-attack/electrocardiogram-ecg-or-ekg

[xxix] https://www.ncbi.nlm.nih.gov/pmc/articles/PMC2772257/

[xxx] Lawrence, 1997, pp. 158-159

[xxxi] Clark, 1984, p. 243

[xxxii] A Near-Death Experience with Veridical Perception Described by a Famous Heart Surgeon and Confirmed by his Assistant Surgeon

Journal of Near-Death Studies, 31(3), Spring 2013, 179-186
[xxxiii] Near-Death and Out-of-Body Experiences in the Blind: A Study of Apparent Eyeless Vision by Kenneth Ring, Ph.D. & Sharon Cooper, M.A. - University of Connecticut
[xxxiv] https://www.youtube.com/watch?v=MFCnPOTCYJE – 1:30
[xxxv] Plato, Phaedo, page 64
[xxxvi] 1 Corinthians 15:53-56
[xxxvii] Deuteronomy 6:4, Mark 12:30
[xxxviii] Isaiah 55:9
[xxxix] Deuteronomy 31:6
[xl] Matthew 11:28-30
[xli] Colossians 1:16-17
[xlii] 1 Corinthians 6:20a
[xliii] Dave paraphrasing some awesome truths
[xliv] Jeremiah 1:5
[xlv] Psalm 139: 13-17
[xlvi] Psalm 4:10a
[xlvii] Revelation 3:20
[xlviii] Psalm 37:4b
[xlix] 1 Corinthians 9:24
[l] Jeremiah 29:11
[li] https://answersingenesis.org/creation-scientists/profiles/johannes-kepler/
[lii] in a letter to Jean-Baptiste Leroy, 1789
[liii] Hebrews 9:27
[liv] Matthew 25:41b
[lv] 2 Peter 3:9
[lvi] 2 Corinthians 5:8
[lvii] Revelation 2:11
[lviii] Genesis 2:17
[lix] 2 Corinthians 1:22
[lx] John 8:44
[lxi] Genesis 3:1b
[lxii] Genesis 3:4
[lxiii] Genesis 3:7b
[lxiv] Genesis 3:21
[lxv] Genesis 3:17
[lxvi] Genesis 3:15
[lxvii] Ephesians 1
[lxviii] Genesis 22:8
[lxix] Revelation 5:12
[lxx] Numbers 6:24-26

Made in the USA
Columbia, SC
26 April 2021